Praise for *We Live for the We*

"Dani McClain reminds us why Black women, specifically Black mothers, are the backbones of every single society. While we are often neglected and disenfranchised, our labor is what has built democracies around the globe. This is a must read for all Black mamas and our allies. Thank you, Dani, and thank you, Dani's daughter, for showing us the way forward."

—Patrisse Khan-Cullors, author of *When They Call You a Terrorist: A Black Lives Matter Memoir*

"Dani McClain charts the rich territory of black motherhood, an element of American life that is overlooked and undervalued even as our society benefits from its tenacity and love. *We Live for the We* is deeply researched, compassionately reported, and soars with the beauty and urgency of McClain's truest expertise: her own life as a black woman raising a young daughter. Parenting is political and we all have much to learn from the work McClain chronicles in these pages. This book is a gift, and it is for everyone."

—Angela Garbes, author of *Like a Mother: A Feminist Journey through the Science and Culture of Pregnancy*

"Dani McClain's *We Live for the We* is more than a reimagining of motherhood. It's an equally soulful and skillful immersion into the questions of how we go beyond survival in a nation intent on the suffering of Black mothers and their children. The book refuses to let us run, every paragraph seeking the contour of who we really are in the dark and how our children will be protected, loved, and tenderly allowed to fail and grow by parents willing to revise what we've all been taught. This is the rare book that will change lives and public policy."

—Kiese Laymon, author of *Heavy: An American Memoir*

"Motherhood is one of the most contested and policed categories that black women occupy in American society. With intellectual gravitas, gifted storytelling, and feminist insights, Dani McClain's *We Live for We* brilliantly chronicles how African-American women confront these contradictions as deeply political and personal acts. This book is a timely, compassionate, and eye-opening contribution to our most pressing debates about race and gender."

—Salamishah Tillet, Henry Rutgers Professor of African American and African Studies and Creative Writing

"*We Live for the We* is a crucial chapter in the history of Black motherhood as a political act. Enslaved mothers taught their babies to read without being discovered, now Black mothers must teach our children to stay safe from police, from sexual predators, from racist teachers. McClain shows that we must be strategic with our rage and still vulnerable with our love—our political work requires this range. This text showcases the harsh realities of Black motherhood and the best solutions currently available, while pointing to the ways we must still change everything for the sake of our children."

—dream hampton, writer, filmmaker, and organizer, and producer of *Surviving R. Kelly*

"Many mothers of my generation lacked safe and effective birth control, survived childhood sexual abuse, or were prematurely sterilized. These experiences shaped our understandings of pregnancy and motherhood. Dani McClain both acknowledges and departs from these painful realities with her portrait of motherhood as an act of liberation. She offers a window into the granularity of the challenges millennials face when parenting. This book describes parenting choices as empowering and bewildering at the same time and, in doing so, portrays the heart of Black mothering."

—Loretta Ross, coauthor of *Reproductive Justice: An Introduction* and cofounder of SisterSong Women of Color Reproductive Justice Collective

"In this generous, well-researched book, Dani McClain bridges realism with idealism, and critique with our shared craving for the better world all of our children deserve. Generations of parents and community members will use this book to make decisions, to revive our hope, and to teach each other about the implications of difference in a stratified society. Most importantly, for me, this book engages and continues the brave multi-generational tradition of Black mothers sharing their own experiences and their revolutionary visions for the benefit of all people. Thank you, Dani McClain, for bringing your hardest questions, your rigorous observations, your priceless relationship with your daughter, and your open heart to this necessary work."

—Alexis Pauline Gumbs, PhD, coeditor of *Revolutionary Mothering: Love on the Front Lines*

"I read this book shouting 'YES!', throwing up praise hands, pacing the floor, overcome with gratitude! *We Live for the We* is a glorious exploration of how we outgrow the isolating terror of oppression and lean into the interdependent wisdom of love. McClain asks questions that require readers to change—change how we think of single parents, of discipline, good births, freedom, education, autonomy, community, safety, and ultimately, power. Conversational and precise, McClain uncovers roots of white supremacy, patriarchy and capitalism in the ground beneath our children's feet. Parents and caregivers of all backgrounds can learn from McClain's deft reporting and storytelling, but Black mothers (and grandis, grammis, grandmas, aunties, sisters, godmothers, midwives, doulas and friends) will learn while also feeling celebrated and loved for how we have lived a legacy of village building, how we have survived the impossible together, and how we are responsible for a thriving Black future."

—adrienne maree brown, author of *Emergent Strategy: Shaping Change, Changing Worlds*, *Pleasure Activism: The Politics of Feeling Good*, and coeditor of *Octavia's Brood: Science Fiction Stories from Social Justice Movements*

"Dani McClain has produced an important work that will show the world just how powerful and transformative radical Black motherhood is and always has been. This path can be very isolating at times but it's refreshing to see that I'm not alone in this process and now other moms, dads, and allies will have the tools to join the fight to make the next generation more self-possessed and feminist than those before them."

—Jamilah Lemieux, writer and cultural critic

"Dani McClain has written that rarest and most satisfying of books—one that illuminates a fraught political and cultural landscape through the pinhole aperture of her own mothering and the questions it surfaces. It is both intimate and epic, sweet and fierce. As a white mother, it read as inspiration and provocation for the kind of parallel questions I need and want to be asking. I'll be a better parent and citizen for having looked through McClain's dynamic lens."

—Courtney E. Martin, author of *The New Better Off: Reinventing the American Dream*

"Dani McClain is one of the most lucid, insightful, and gifted critics working today: her work sings with eloquence and is driven by analytical fury. This is the book we parents need right now!"

—Michael Eric Dyson, author of *What Truth Sounds Like: Robert F. Kennedy, James Baldwin, and Our Unfinished Conversation about Race in America*

We Live for the We

We Live for the We

The Political Power of Black Motherhood

Dani McClain

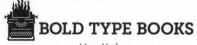

BOLD TYPE BOOKS

New York

Bold Type Books
116 East 16th Street, 8th Floor New York, NY 10003
www.boldtypebooks.org
@BoldTypeBooks
Printed in the United States of America

First Edition: April 2019

Published by Bold Type Books, an imprint of Perseus Books, LLC, a subsidiary of Hachette Book Group, Inc. Bold Type Books is a co-publishing venture of the Type Media Center and Perseus Books.

The Hachette Speakers Bureau provides a wide range of authors for speaking events. To find out more, go to www.hachettespeakersbureau.com or call (866) 376-6591.

The publisher is not responsible for websites (or their content) that are not owned by the publisher.

Print book interior design by Amnet Systems.

Library of Congress Cataloging in Publication Control Number: 2018053975

ISBNs: 978-1-56858-854-4 (hardcover); 978-1-56858-855-1 (e-book)

LSC-C

10 9 8 7 6 5 4 3 2 1

To Andrea McClain
and
In memory of Pamela Suzanne McClain

Raising black children—female and male—in the mouth of a racist, sexist, suicidal dragon is perilous and chancy. If they cannot love and resist at the same time, they will probably not survive.

—AUDRE LORDE, "MAN CHILD," *SISTER OUTSIDER:*
ESSAYS AND SPEECHES (1984)

Contents

Introduction

WHEN I WAS SEVEN OR EIGHT YEARS OLD, MY MOTHER PUT ON WHITNEY Houston's recording of "Greatest Love of All" every day before we left home for school and work, and we sang along from start to finish. We stood in the living room in those moments before we shrugged on our coats and belted out lyrics about self-reliance and refusing to let the possibility of failure keep us from trying. We wrapped ourselves in the richness and power of Whitney's voice, reaching for the high notes right along with her. I can't remember how long this lasted. It could've been weeks or even months, but I remember it as a defining ritual of my childhood. We weren't much of a singing family, but in the mid-1980s, my mother made sure we shrouded ourselves in a kind of armor through song and remembered who we were before facing a day that was sure to challenge us.

She's too young now, but I plan to do something similar with my daughter, Isobel, who has just turned two at the time of this writing. For her, I might build a ritual around

Nina Simone's "To Be Young, Gifted and Black" or maybe
the Donny Hathaway version. Black children and their families need this, I think. We need a kind of anthem, a melodic
reminder to ourselves and each other that we are not who the
wider world too often tells us we are: criminal, disposable,
lazy, undeserving of health or peace or laughter.

This book is about my quest as a new mother to help my
daughter understand as early as possible who she is and what
she came to do on this beleaguered planet. It reflects on our
experiences in the first years of her life and weaves together
interviews with black mothers and grandmothers who are
further along this journey and generous with their stories of
triumphs and tribulations. I have chosen to focus on mothers rather than parents more broadly, because my reporting
was driven by my most urgent questions. I am black, and I
am a woman. These aspects of my identity will shape how
I guide my daughter. Throughout the book, I sometimes
choose the verb "to mother" over the noun "motherhood," an
approach I learned from Alexis Pauline Gumbs, China Martens, and Mai'a Williams, coeditors of the book *Revolutionary
Mothering*. Mothering is an action done by a range of people,
including grandmothers, aunts, and queer and gender nonconforming people who don't identify as women but who see
themselves engaging in, as Gumbs puts it, "the practice of creating, nurturing, affirming and supporting life."[1]

This book sets out to broaden a conversation established
by the current wave of writing on motherhood, which has
tended to focus on white, middle-class women's experiences.
These writings frame motherhood as something that robs

women of our professional ambitions, gets us off track as earners, and reminds us that biology and age-old gender roles are indeed destiny. I can relate to funny anecdotes about sleep deprivation, toddlers' antics, and ruined sex lives, but these articles and books rarely address the politics of mothering—namely, issues of power, position, and protection.

I know that motherhood is deeply political. Black women are more likely to die during pregnancy or birth than women of any other race. I endured health problems during my pregnancy and had only white medical providers, so I've thought a lot about the link between bias in health care and maternal mortality. My own mother, who has never married and who worked full-time throughout my childhood, is a model for my own parenting. But culture war messages—from the left and the right—tell us she fell short of maternal ideals. My grandmother, great-grandmother, aunts, and elders in the community supported my mother as she raised me. Their investment in me and in other children—some their blood relations, some not—demonstrated an ethic of care and mutual aid that we can all learn from.

For this book, I spoke with mothers who have ties to movements for social, political, and cultural change. I sought them out because I found it likely that they had at some point grappled with the questions I am facing as a new parent. They are parents to young children and parents to grown-ups. They are parents to siblings and to only children. They are partnered and single. They include educators and health workers, academics and retirees, artists and spiritual guides, a therapist, a city planner, and many organizers and activists.

The title, *We Live for the We*, is something one of these mothers, Cat Brooks, often tells her twelve-year-old daughter when their individual desires come up against some larger community need. "Our job as black mothers is to keep pushing the liberation ball down the court. Our obligation is to leave the world better for them and to ensure that they are equipped with the tools that they need to fight," Brooks, an organizer in Oakland, told me when I interviewed her. "I tell my daughter all the time—and it's harsh—but we don't live for the I. We live for the we."

With her words, Brooks brought contemporary meaning to something I'd read in scholarship on black motherhood. Historically, black women have engaged in what sociologist Patricia Hill Collins has called "other-mothering," a system of care through which they are accountable to and work on behalf of all black children in a particular community. This broad understanding of family responsibility often became a launch pad for public service. Collins writes, "For many women, what began as the daily expression of their obligations as community other-mothers . . . developed into full-fledged roles as community leaders."[2]

In addition to serving as other-mothers, we've had to fight for our right to be mothers. Prior to emancipation, enslaved people could not lay legal claim to their children.[3] The child of an enslaved woman was someone's property. For the more than four hundred years since the inception of slavery on this continent, black women have had to inhabit a different understanding of motherhood in order to navigate American life. If we merely accepted the status quo and failed to challenge the forces that have kept black people and women oppressed, then we participated in our own and our children's destruction.

This has been especially evident in recent years as dozens of black women and men have had to stand before television cameras telling the world that their recently slain children were in fact human beings, were in fact loved and sources of joy, despite whatever stories law enforcement or conservative media were telling about why they deserved their untimely deaths. In these moments, I've been reminded of how much is asked of black parents and of how politically powerful black parenting can be. The mothers of those killed by police or vigilante violence embody every black mother's deepest fears: that we will not be able to adequately protect our children from or prepare them for a world that has to be convinced of their worth. Many parents speak of feeling more fear and anxiety once they take responsibility for keeping another human alive and well. But black women especially know fear—how to live despite it and how to metabolize it for our children so they're not consumed by it.

In the pages that follow, I show how one black American mother is reimagining what it means to parent during a time of conservative backlash, growing authoritarian tendencies, and a rise in white supremacist and patriarchal violence and rhetoric. This book explores how to raise a black girl child in the age of #BlackLivesMatter and #MeToo. At two, my daughter is already full of questions, and I wonder what she'll ask me as she gets older. I wonder how the world will change in these coming decades, how we'll experience shifts in climate, whether US institutions and our confidence in them will continue to collapse. I wonder if I'll be around to watch with her as we collectively pull ourselves back from the brink of extinction and bring about a renaissance, a social reordering that benefits more of us. I also wonder just how bad things can get and how soon—how our family will manage if we find ourselves in a postapocalyptic landscape similar to something out of an Octavia Butler novel. Whatever our fate, how will I answer her questions about how things were when she was a baby? How will I explain the choices I've made as an individual, the choices made by the communities we belong to, the choices made by the governments and corporations that have so much influence over our lives?

What has been interesting, in the fever dream that has been life in the United States since Donald Trump came to power, is that some of black women's deepest fears have become more comprehensible to the broader society. Those who believed they had no real reason to doubt that their children would be safe in this country are increasingly terrified. Things they felt they could take for granted before the 2016 election—that our leaders generally agreed that antagonizing a nuclear power with childish Twitter provocations was a bad idea; that despite climate change and environmental toxins, at least some smart and ethical people were empowered to fight the good fight at the EPA; or that democracy and its attendant norms would keep the United States stable—are no longer a given. No one has ever been able to guarantee safe passage into adulthood for their children, but nonblack parents with money, citizenship, and class status had a leg up on the rest of us. Now, even for many of them, the threats and uncertainty seem to multiply by the day. The Trump era, it seems, has given those who may have previously felt invulnerable to the shifting tides of human fortune a wake-up call.

At a time when "Resist!" has for some become a national battle cry in response to the norms-trampling Trump administration, it's critical to look at the messages communicated within our families and address any hypocrisies or inconsistencies head on. I don't think it's possible to be ready for the tough questions my own daughter will ask someday, but I know I want to be available for them. Family is often the first social institution to shape how we understand our identities and our politics.[4] We should all seize the opportunity, and the mothers whose words appear on the pages that follow can act as guides.

The research suggests that white parents in particular need help with seeing family as a site of political education, especially when it comes to passing on antiracist values. A 2007 study in the *Journal of Marriage and Family* found that out of seventeen thousand families with kindergartners, parents of color are about three times more likely to discuss race than their white counterparts. Seventy-five percent of the white parents in the study never or almost never talked about race. According to research highlighted in Po Bronson and Ashley Merryman's 2009 book, *NurtureShock*, white parents communicate messages that skin color doesn't matter and that everyone is equal, messages children know to be lies based on their own experiences even as early as infancy. When pressed, these parents often admit that they don't know how to talk about race and are scared that if they try, their kids will say the wrong things in the world.[5]

Black mothers, on the other hand, are scared not of *talk* of race but of the impact of racist oppression. We're scared because we have no choice but to release our beloved creations into environments—doctor's offices, hospitals, daycare facilities, playgrounds, schools—where white supremacy is often woven into the fabric of the institution and is both consciously and unwittingly practiced by the people acting in loco parentis. Black mothers haven't had the luxury of sticking our heads in the sand and hoping our children learn about race and power as they go. Instead, we must act as a buffer and translator between them and the world, beginning from their earliest days.

We Live for the We is structured around the questions mothers ask at each stage of a child's life. The first three chapters focus on matters that consume us early on: How will I give birth? What kind of home does this child need? What will family mean to this child? The next three chapters focus on socialization and education. The final three chapters focus on questions we may think of as relevant to older children: How do I introduce religion or spirituality? How and when should we talk about sex? How should we talk about politics, and when is the right time to bring her along to rallies, protests, and marches?

Of course, there are gaps in my reporting that other books will need to focus on. Many sources, like me, experience privilege on the basis of our education and class status. I don't address the challenges of parenting while homeless or while incarcerated, nor do I address the child welfare system, a mechanism of surveillance and control that affects the lives of too many black mothers who are punished because their poverty is read as neglect.

My desire to research how black mothers talk to their children about their bodies and sexual health, the focus of Chapter 7, grew out of the six years I've spent reporting on the reproductive justice movement. The book in its entirety is guided by the intellectual framework reproductive justice offers—that the right to parent children in safe and healthy environments is just as critical as the right to abortion and contraception. I am indebted to Loretta Ross, a reproductive justice foremother whom I have interviewed over the years, and activists on the front lines who have patiently pointed me in the direction of important stories and sources.

The words and actions of many scholars, journalists, and organizers inspired me to embark on this project: Patricia Hill Collins, bell hooks, and Audre Lorde are quoted throughout. I leaned heavily on Stacey Patton's book on black families and discipline in reporting Chapter 2. I had Nikole Hannah-Jones's education coverage in mind as I formulated the questions at the heart of Chapter 6. I have long been an admirer of Trina Greene Brown, founder of the organization Parenting for Liberation. Her words below, shared with me during a January 2018 interview, are a perfect invitation into the pages that follow:

> We are raising children who were never meant to survive . . . People who are raising kids who *were* meant to survive have a lot to learn from us. We can teach resilience.

We can instill pride. We can instill values around compassion and love. We can also instill a sense of joy and play in horrible conditions . . . You have a lot to learn from the magic of Black mothering and Black parenting. Imagine what we could do if we actually had resources. Imagine what we could do if we actually were on fertile soil and not in a desert. Imagine if it wasn't concrete and we were planting roses. Just imagine what would be possible.

CHAPTER 1

Birth

It's a Sunday afternoon in July 2016, and I'm lying on my bed, trying to calm down. The month's rapid-fire events are hitting me square in the gut. Today, someone agitated by police shootings of black men ambushed police in Baton Rouge. Already, commentators are pointing a finger at black organizers. Just over a week ago, a Black Lives Matter protest in Dallas ended with a sniper targeting police there; in return, the police circulated an image of an innocent protester as a suspect before using a robot to kill the alleged perpetrator. Two days before the Dallas shooting, Baton Rouge police killed Alton Sterling while he was pinned to the ground, and the next day Philando Castile was shot dead by police during a traffic stop in a suburb of St. Paul, Minnesota, while his girlfriend and her four-year-old daughter sat inches away.

For the past three years, my job has been to report on black-led organizing and the police violence that fuels it, and until recently, I've been able to read and process related news with the detachment that my journalism training has

instilled in me. But now, what I see online and on TV simply makes me afraid. I am seven months pregnant, and these
days, tragic events hit me in a way that I can't neatly tuck away.
I'm learning that in moments like these, it's critical that I step
away from the screen and stop crying, that I figure out how
to return my breathing to normal. My health and my fetus's
health depend on it.

Black women, after all, are almost four times more likely
to die from pregnancy complications than our white counterparts, and black babies are twice as likely as white babies
to die before their first birthday. I worry that I'll have a baby
that's too small to thrive or that I'll be treated so negligently
by the hospital staff during delivery that I will end up seriously injured or dead.

I shouldn't have to worry. I eat a healthy diet; I don't
have high blood pressure or diabetes. I am not poor; I have
private insurance and a master's degree. I started prenatal
appointments at ten weeks and haven't missed one. But
I'm under no illusion that my class privilege will save me.
Research suggests that it's the stress caused by racial discrimination experienced over a lifetime that leads to black
American women's troubling birth outcomes, not the individual choices those women make or how much money or
education they have.

I have sat slack-jawed as I read the work of public health
researcher Arline Geronimus, who has found that the average black woman might be less healthy at twenty-five than
she was at fifteen and that African American women at

thirty-five have the rates of disability of white Americans who are fifty-five. The American experience tears away at the black body. I am thirty-eight years old, and so daily slights and structural racism have had plenty of time to take their toll.

Thus my decision that day, made during the long summer of my third trimester, to take a break from the news, which served as a constant reminder of two disturbing realities: One, that in carrying a black child, I was carrying a potential Sterling or Castile or Rekia Boyd or Tamir Rice. And two, that my health and that of my child-to-be were largely in the hands of people who, like me, had been watching events unfold in Baton Rouge or Dallas or Ferguson or Chicago—but who may have had a completely different understanding from me of how race works in this country.

When I walked into my ob-gyn's office in Dayton, Ohio, or into the offices of the various specialists I saw over the course of my pregnancy, I suspected that the all-white teams of receptionists, nurses, and doctors (OK, there was a black receptionist at the office where I got my ultrasounds) first saw a black woman, not an Ivy League graduate or someone whose job included researching reproductive health—or any of the other characteristics that some may think would shield me from substandard care. An Institute of Medicine report found that people of color "are less likely to receive needed services" even when their insurance and income are the same as white people's.[1] So I tried to leverage every bit of privilege I could to stave off any assumptions that my health-care providers might have made. I wasn't married and rarely wore my engagement ring, but I made sure to put it on before every prenatal appointment. When I showed up to an appointment with cornrows or an Afro, I wondered if I'd be treated differently from the times I'd come with my hair flat-ironed.

These concerns may seem far-fetched, but during my pregnancy, they were very real to me. A 2016 study by the University of Virginia found that about half of the white medical students and residents surveyed held at least one false belief about biological differences between black and white people: that black people's nerve endings are less sensitive than white people's, for instance. These were not randomly selected people, mind you, but students well on their way to becoming doctors. Those implicit biases affected their ability to make appropriate decisions about treating black patients. Dr. Norman Oliver, a coauthor of the study and Virginia's current state health commissioner, told me that while the so-called social determinants of health—access to safe housing, jobs, education, health insurance—are largely responsible for health inequities, bias in clinical treatment also plays a role. A 1999 study of cardiovascular health found that black women are at a particular disadvantage when it comes to receiving adequate care.[2]

Speaking to Oliver made me think of the minutes before my daughter's birth late that summer of 2016, when the nurse in charge of administering the anesthetic introduced himself to me just prior to my C-section. He was a white man, friendly, willing to answer all of my questions. When he finished explaining the process we were about to begin, I looked him in the eyes and made him promise me that I wouldn't feel anything, as if personal obligation rather than his training would get me the appropriate care. I didn't need to read Oliver's research to fear that I might feel my obstetrician slice into my abdomen due to racist ideas about pain and blackness.

This same distrust caused me to be skeptical that I actually needed the C-section I was told was necessary at fourteen weeks. That's when a white doctor reviewed my ultrasound and told me that not only did I have fibroids but also that the largest one—the size of a grapefruit—was blocking the birth canal, making vaginal birth impossible. That doctor had also been warm and responsive, but the encounter—especially her warning that the fibroids put me at increased risk for hemorrhage and hysterectomy during surgery—set me on edge. I hadn't known prior to the ultrasound that I had fibroids, but I had many friends and family members who did have them; black women are up to three times more likely than white women to have them. I knew that the C-section rate in the United States—32 percent—is more than double what's recommended by the World Health Organization. The C-section rate here is slightly higher for black women than for white women, even for black women who are low-risk. Was I being steered by a provider with unconscious racial bias toward becoming another statistic? I held on to the possibility that she and my white obstetrician, who confirmed her findings, were wrong, that they couldn't imagine the same options for me that they might for a white patient.

It wasn't until I'd gotten a second opinion from a black woman ob-gyn that I accepted that a C-section was the right choice. I felt more confident that she'd been able to see me as a human being, just like her.

ॐ

ANAYAH SANGODELE-AYOKA, A CERTIFIED NURSE MID-wife, tells me that this desire for what she calls cultural congruence is common among the patients she sees. The Washington, DC, hospital where she works hosts an event where expectant families can hear from all eleven of the midwives available to work with them. At the end of these events, the black families in attendance will line up to talk one-on-one with Sangodele-Ayoka, who is one of two black midwives in the practice. "People generally want someone who's more familiar," she tells me. "They want to know that somebody is going to understand the concerns that they have around racialized trauma, around bringing kids into the world, around family dynamics."

Sangodele-Ayoka has found that with an increased level of comfort, her patients are more willing to open up about issues that are relevant to their health but that may be received differently and with more judgment by a nonblack provider. For example, an expecting mom may admit that she and her partner fight or that she uses marijuana or that the family doesn't have enough to eat. Once Sangodele-Ayoka has a more complete picture of that pregnant person's life, she can offer tailored support, including interventions aimed at reducing stress.

"Let's take some deep breaths. Let's talk about what it's like to be a black woman," she tells me, offering examples of how a conversation with a patient might go. She'll tell that patient how pressures from family, from work, and from the world can affect her nervous system and thus her birth. They might talk about how to set better boundaries or how to do a yoga pose that offers physical relief from the discomforts of pregnancy. She often finds herself convincing her patients that taking care of themselves isn't at all selfish. It's actually necessary.

Black birth workers—midwives as well as doulas, who assist but provide no medical care—can encourage health and self-determination in black parents-to-be. They can also help black families navigate inhospitable health-care settings. Linda Jones has been a birth and postpartum doula in the San Francisco Bay Area for nearly thirty years. Jones, who is black, says her clients of color are treated differently by medical staff. White couples are assumed to be married; other couples are not. A standard question about drug and alcohol use is often glossed over for white couples. Part of Jones's job is to prepare her clients for what to expect while at doctors' appointments or during a hospital birth, arming them with questions for providers. "They need someone to help empower them to have the birth that they want," Jones said. "If we can get women-of-color doulas and women-of-color midwives, the trauma will lessen," she told me. "Maybe we'll stop dying and maybe we'll stop having all these C-sections that seem to be our lot."

I have no problem asking doctors questions, even to the point of making a nuisance of myself. Still, I considered hiring a doula for the birth. I would have preferred a black woman, but at the time I couldn't find one in southwestern Ohio. Black women in particular have an unmet need for birth assistance, according to a 2016 Choices in Childbirth report. Of the black women surveyed, 39 percent wanted but did not have access to the services of a doula, compared with 30 percent of Latinas and 22 percent of white women.[3] I interviewed a white woman for the job and liked her well enough, but her services cost $900, and my partner and I didn't want to pay that much; we were already paying $200 for a birth-education course through a local hospital.

In addition to offering general information on labor and birth, the course, called Hypnobirthing, emphasizes a relaxation method that involves positive visualizations. I was less interested in that than in being part of a community of first-time parents who, like my partner and me, had questions about everything from the best positions for labor to what an epidural does. Out of about a dozen couples in the class, we were one of two black couples. There was also a Latino couple, and the rest appeared to be of European descent. The teacher was a white woman, and so were all the guest speakers she brought in over the course of the eight-week class. During some of the sessions, the instructor showed a lack of sensitivity to the issues that mattered to me. A handout on the reasons one might have a surgical birth omitted fibroids but included high blood pressure, breech positioning, and herpes. When I brought up fibroids, I was met with a roomful of blank stares. We were told that the number-one reason for preterm birth is dehydration. Among black women, 16 percent deliver babies before they're full-term—and that's simply because we're not drinking enough water?

When I checked in with black midwives, doulas, and obstetricians across the country, they all pointed to something like an improved version of this class—a circle of support that's culturally competent—as critical to improving the birth outcomes for black American women. Circles can take many different forms. In April 2016, Detroit's Henry Ford Health System began piloting a project that offers group prenatal care to women at high risk for preterm labor. Groups of no more than a dozen women who were in the same trimester met for two hours monthly. In the first half hour, they got one-on-one clinical care: their blood pressure and weight were checked, their bellies measured. They spent the rest of the time with each other in a conversation facilitated by a certified nurse midwife and a community health worker. The women also got home visits from the health worker, who made sure, for example, they had solid housing and access to transportation or could get out of violent relationships. As of mid-December of that year, women who had gone through the pilot had given birth to twenty-five babies, Kimberlydawn Wisdom, the senior vice president of community health and equity at Henry Ford Health System, told me. Only one baby had been under a healthy weight. None were sent to the neonatal intensive care unit. None of the mothers were sent to the ICU. One hundred percent of the moms had started breastfeeding and were connected to lactation consultants.

A previous version of the initiative simply connected expecting women with the community health worker. None of the more than three hundred women who participated in that earlier program had experienced an infant death, said Wisdom, who's led both efforts to tackle infant mortality. Wisdom said the community health workers help combat the poverty-related stress participants face. "You've got somebody you can call," she said. "It's been very empowering to these women."

For Sangodele-Ayoka, the DC-based midwife, a group model of prenatal care could allow her to provide services to the families she serves in the communities where they live. In 2017, two hospital obstetrics units east of the Anacostia River closed their doors. They had served primarily low-income black and Latina women, and left the city with a maternity-care desert.[4] Now, families who live east of the river have to travel twenty minutes by car or an hour on public transit to deliver their babies. The hospital where Sangodele-Ayoka works is downtown, just ten minutes from the White House, and now serves some of these women. But when we speak in September 2018, she's working on a proposal to launch a new program that would allow these families to stay closer to home for care leading up to their birth. As she sees it, the group approach allows the typical power dynamic—health provider at the top of the hierarchy and participants as empty vessels into whom information is poured—to dissolve. More peer-to-peer sharing can take place. Any standard instruction can happen fairly quickly, leaving plenty of time for conversations about more nuanced topics that ob-gyns often ignore, like perineal massage and breastfeeding.

Jamarah Amani, a Florida-based midwife, runs the Southern Birth Justice Network and sees midwifery care specifically as a key to closing the racial disparities in pregnancy and birth. "Folks become part of a circle of mamas," she tells me of a group she works with in Miami. "It's sort of a rite of passage and an entryway into this community of parenting." Through participation in the circle, a woman is connected to doulas, lactation consultants, pediatricians, government-funded early childhood services, and other resources. When a family works with a midwife, Amani tells me, they're entering a different type of relationship than they would be entering with an obstetrician. She sees it as part of her job to know the full picture of how the women she works with are doing—emotionally, spiritually, financially. For example, she knows who lives in a food desert and so lacks access to the food she needs to have a healthy pregnancy.

Before training to become a midwife, Amani was a community organizer who worked on reproductive health as well as racial and economic justice. Her long-standing work with marginalized communities gives her the perspective she needs to be a good midwife for low-income women and women of color. "The more [birth] professionals we see who are social justice oriented and community grounded, we will see changes in those disparities," she tells me.

Tamika Middleton is an Atlanta-based doula. In 2007, she birthed her son at home with the help of a black midwife. When she found out she was pregnant, she had recently moved to Atlanta from New Orleans in the wake of Hurricane Katrina and had just started graduate school. She checked out several hospital-based midwifery practices and was turned away because they didn't accept Medicaid. Then a nurse referred her to the woman who would eventually support her home birth. What this midwife, who is black, offered was something we're hard-pressed to find in a doctor's office: time and deep relationship. Middleton says she would come over, and they would spend hours together, watching birth videos and talking. "She didn't have a problem with me asking a billion questions if I had them," Middleton says. They got to know each other's families. They did a childbirth education class together. "She brought me into this community of other [black and Latina] women who had had home births as well and other midwives. They had dinners and gatherings and birthday parties, and we were all there."

She contrasts her pregnancy to that of two cousins who were pregnant at the same time and preparing for hospital births. When they all compared notes, it was clear that the hours at a stretch that Middleton spent with her midwife left her better informed, so she became a kind of birth educator for her family. One cousin's conversations with her doctor about her weight made her stressed and ashamed, Middleton says, which dampened her ability to communicate well with her provider. "There was some trauma from the experience, some sadness that I had not experienced with my birth. That's part of what inspired me to become a doula, because I was able to see how different the care was between a midwife and a hospital."

After my own daughter's birth, I meet a black, Ohio-based doula who could have attended my birth, had we been able to find one another. But Denise Thomas hadn't turned up in my Google searches. She's what she calls a "church doula."

People usually find her through word of mouth, and most of her clients are fellow congregants at the church she attends. We meet at a Starbucks in Dayton, where Thomas lives, and from its parking lot I can see the hospital where my daughter, Is, was born. Thomas has been a certified doula for the past decade, and she emphasizes what I've learned from others I've talked to: black birth workers give freely of their time, doing whatever they can to meet their clients' needs and lessen their stress.

Thomas knows what it is to be pregnant and need help. She was on months-long bedrest twice, once while pregnant with her seventeen-year-old daughter and again with her fifteen-year-old twins. Her husband was supportive, as were her mother and sister, but they all worked. She needed additional help with laundry, cooking, and cleaning. "You don't want to ask for help," she says, connecting her own experience with those of the women she works with. "We've got a superwoman chip on our shoulder. We do stuff without even thinking about it, because we're natural-born caregivers. It's like, 'I got it.' No, you don't." Thomas says in situations like these, money is the last thing on her mind. "I'll step in and do stuff without even asking for payment," she tells me. "Like, 'Hey, I'm coming over. Girl, what you doing over here? Let me help you with this.' I'll just jump in."

Thomas charges about $450 for her services but will doula for free if need be. If more insurance companies covered doulas, that would help, she says. As it is, her clients have to pay her out of pocket and then try to get insurance companies to reimburse them, which rarely happens. All the midwives and

doulas I spoke to talked about offering sliding scales, barter-
ing, and otherwise doing what they can to make their services
accessible to the women they want to serve. Herself a mother
of four, Amani (of Miami) says keeping the commitment can
cause a financial strain. "I am often faced with that question . . .
How much am I giving away? I think a lot of midwives who
are grounded in their communities are."

The challenges of staying afloat financially are one reason
so few black birth workers are able to enter and stay in the
field. Fewer than 2 percent of midwives in the United States
are black.[5] Amani gives context for the state where she works.
"There were close to four thousand midwives in Florida at the
turn of the twentieth century, and now we have under two
hundred," she tells me. "The overwhelming majority of those
three thousand plus were black, and now the overwhelming
majority of those two hundred are white."

Progressive-era public health reforms contributed to this
tremendous shift. Midwives and home births predate doctors
and hospitals. But with the rise of the latter, public health
campaigns often demonized midwives as being dirty and
ignorant, an undesirable option if a hospital birth attended
by a doctor was available. Because of new regulations, midwives were often driven out of business or placed under the
supervision of doctors and nurses. In some states, including
North Carolina, where Sangodele-Ayoka has practiced, midwives even today need a collaborative agreement with a doctor
signing off as a kind of endorsement allowing the midwife to
practice. "You find it mostly in southern states," she tells me.
"It's a relic of patriarchy. It's a relic of sexism."

Getting the education and certification that allows a midwife to practice in a broad range of settings, including hospitals, is another barrier that keeps marginalized people from thriving in the field. There are certified nurse midwives, who get degrees in nursing and then go on to graduate programs for midwifery. There are direct-entry midwives, who are not nurses but have training and in some cases licensure, depending on the state requirements where they live. Then there are lay or traditional midwives, who learn the craft through apprenticeship, can attend home births, and generally operate underground.[6] The overwhelming majority of black midwives fall into this last group. Add to this hierarchy the challenge of finding opportunities where a midwife-in-training can get experience attending births. "One of the biggest barriers is finding a preceptor," Amani tells me, using another word for the clinical training. "Some of those sites are not open to having people of color. Some of them are far, so you have to move there." The profession demands that trainees be on call and so available around the clock, which makes taking on other work difficult.

Since 2016, Jennie Joseph, a midwife, has run a clinic in an African American neighborhood that includes one of Orlando's worst zip codes for perinatal health. Her clinic has attracted national attention for her work addressing health disparities. In 2006 and 2007, Joseph conducted a study with the Health Council of East Central Florida that enrolled one hundred women who would go on to have hospital births. None of the African American or Latina women had a low-weight or preterm baby. Joseph told me it's what happens in her clinic, from the front desk to the examination room, that erases racial disparities. Her clinic accepts people who are denied care elsewhere for a variety of reasons, often because something's gone wrong with their Medicaid application or because they're underinsured or undocumented. Too often, the humiliation that poor women experience keeps them from getting care. "What we do is operate the front desk as a triage desk," Joseph said. "It's financial; it's social; it's 'What's your problem, honey? We'll fix it. We're going to listen to your baby right now.'"

Once a woman knows that she won't be turned away, she's more likely to trust her provider, open up, and comply with any instructions she's given. Joseph said she sees an inability to connect to the fetus in utero as a problem for black women in particular and a reason why preterm birth is so common for them. If a woman is afraid that she can't keep her child-to-be safe, she needs help managing her anxieties. Just like me on the bed that July afternoon, she needs help calming down.

Deciding to turn away from news events made my own pregnancy easier, as did the family members and friends who sheltered me from the stressors of the world. And despite my initial misgivings, my white male obstetrician was consistently thoughtful and patient during our appointments. He showed me real kindness and made good on his promise that no matter what time I went into labor, he'd be there. That moment came on a Thursday evening when my partner and I were headed out for dinner and a movie. I was exhausted and uncomfortable but determined not to let my sciatica or weeks of insomnia keep us from seeing *Southside with You,* about the Obamas' first date. I sat in the car while he went inside a Moroccan restaurant to order our food. Suddenly warm water gushed from my body, and I realized, "Oh. This is it." After returning home to grab our packed bags, we made our way to the hospital, ready to meet our baby.

Because I had a C-section, it's all a bit of a medicated blur, but I remember in those hours after Is's birth seeing in her face hints of the same expressions I see there today—the skepticism, the seriousness. As soon as I went into labor, my beloved friend of twenty years got on the road and drove from Detroit to be our doula. She was there to meet the three of us as we came out of the operating room. Parents, aunts, and uncles would join us in the hours that followed, and there would be what felt like a constant coming and going of nurses and doctors, asking questions, administering tests, coaching me on breastfeeding, leaving documents by the bed to sign.

Within hours of Is's birth, it began to sink in that this small person was no longer part of my body and that I couldn't control everything that happened to her. She was a separate being. And so began the lessons in letting go. So began my lessons in mothering.

CHAPTER 2

Home

I HAVE DECIDED THAT THE MOST IMPORTANT SITE OF STRUGGLE IS IN MY home and, more specifically, in my kitchen. That is where I prepare my daughter's food, putting in the time it takes to avoid the processed, the poisoned, the unpronounceable. I want to give Is healthy, nutrient-rich meals, and so food preparation and cleanup have become among the most time-consuming parts of my daily schedule. While I cook or wash dishes or unload the dishwasher, I talk to her about what she's watching me do. The kitchen is where I nurse her, aware that some people have negative opinions about breastfeeding a child her age. The kitchen is also where I read my daughter book after book, switching up pronouns where necessary to create equal opportunities for women, girls, and nongendered protagonists. I notice the gap and make this intervention even before I read that of the one hundred most popular children's picture books of 2017, a fifth lacked female characters entirely, and the majority were dominated by male characters, often in stereotypically masculine roles.[1]

At the urging of a friend who visits and notices immediately that the kitchen is the heart of our home, I move my desk into a corner there. Now I can quickly respond to an email or look up something while Is naps in her room, within earshot of the kitchen. After her first birthday, she becomes more interested in picture books, and I keep a stash of them—mostly gifts from friends—there, lining the top of my desk so that I can pull one down and read to her at the kitchen table. The nearly indestructible board books are fine scattered across the floor or on a shelf in her room that she can reach herself, but not these.

Sometimes I am aware that the world outside is whizzing past me and that I'm doing very little to engage it or participate in its warp-speed conversations, set to the crazed tempo of this current administration. In 2016, just after Trump's election, the *Chicago Reader* interviewed journalist Jamie Kalven, who broke the story of Laquan McDonald, the sixteen-year-old black boy killed by Chicago police. Kalven said of the moment, "One of the dangers is that people will instead become demoralized and retreat into denial, that they will seek refuge amid the pleasures and fulfillments of private life. . . . There was a term used in central Europe to describe those who opted to retreat into private life under totalitarianism. They were called 'internal emigres.'"[2]

Whether because of this political moment or simply because I now have a young child, it's true that I've retreated into private life. I've slowed way down, turned inward. I've long been interested in nutrition, but now my research on the topic and the food prep I do as a result feels all-consuming.

I read about the impact of nutrition on brain development in the first two years of a child's life and learn that my daughter's mental health, as well as her likelihood of developing obesity, hypertension, and diabetes, may all be programmed by her nutrition during these first thousand days of life.[3]

I start noticing how much I and the other adults in her life are on our phones around Is. I buy an analog clock for the kitchen, so I won't have to touch my phone whenever I need to know the time. The clock doesn't reduce my phone dependence by much. I still use it to check weather, play music, and keep an eye on email. I've never been a big social media user, but I cut back even more and reserve most of my scrolling for after Is goes to sleep. I'm in the midst of fine-tuning these daily practices at home when I read a blog post from a New Orleans–based writer named Lydia Nichols in which she frames this slowing down as characteristic of what she calls anti-imperialist parenting. Nichols writes, "To exercise independence from the state, loosening our dependence on the conveniences it grants us, requires time, a luxury that a lot of parents, particularly those at the intersections of being black, Indigenous, poor, and/or woman, don't have. Across the board, including in our child-rearing, we're encouraged to save time to maximize our labor capacity, from spanking to microwaving meals, often with no thought about how these actions are born of our experiences as subjects of the Imperialist state and how they will shape our children's relationships with the Imperialist state."[4]

I like that she identifies the politics in what I'm trying to do. My no-screens, no-pesticides, no-sexist-books standards are not early signs that I'll be an annoying, obsessive helicopter parent. These standards are my way of trying to exercise independence not from the state necessarily but from a path of least resistance I'm sure will lead our family someplace I don't want us to go. As Nichols points out, I know that my ability to focus so squarely on my daughter is a luxury afforded to few. Is's health and happiness are my priority, and when I am feeling guilty or wondering what's happened to my ambition, I tell myself that I am claiming this time with my daughter as something bigger, something historically meaningful and due me and black women as a whole. It is, in fact, a form of reparations. (Though I am doing this on my own dime. Real reparations would look more like the generous subsidized parental leave offered in some European countries.) I am claiming for myself and my child time that was historically denied black women and children who wanted and needed to bond. I am taking the time that so many black women before me could not, because they were caring for someone else's child or cooking someone else's food or toiling away in someone else's field. The specifics may have changed, but the conditions persist: Most of us still cannot take this precious time with our young ones.

My own mother went back to her retail job six weeks after my birth. I was born near the end of May, and she remembers her boss asking if she could come back to work the Fourth of July sale. She left me in the care of her own mother. Her grandmother cared for me when I was an infant, too. My earliest memories of home are rooted in feeling, in the senses. I remember the ever-present smell of good food cooking.

I remember lots of laughter and jokes with Mom's youngest sister, who was a teenager when I was born and always around. I remember playing dress-up with my cousins. I remember my grandparents, aunts and uncles, and family friends setting up card tables and playing bid whist into the night. I remember feeling that these were my people and this was my place, that I belonged among them.

I want Is to have a strong grounding in a place that feels safe, comfortable, calm, and consistent. I want to create for her an oasis, a protected space where she can learn who she is and how to be. By paying a high level of attention to her food, books, and other sensory stimulation, I am trying to provide the best environment and inputs possible—just as I did for myself during my pregnancy—so that she's not starting at a deficit. But I'm trying to accomplish something else in shaping her early understandings of home. I also want our home to be a microcosm of the world I want to live in, a place where kindness, compassion, and justice are valued and consistently worked toward.

If I'm establishing a protected space, what exactly am I protecting my child from? Why is it that the outside world has become not just less interesting but also a place where it seems something terrifying lurks around every corner? In reading the work of other new mothers, I find that I'm not alone. Many parents experience a heightened fear that shapes our relationship with our children, distorts our perceptions, and creates a kind of vulnerability that verges on physical sensation. I come across a white mother's account and feel a wave of recognition. In the magazine *Tin House*, Alyssa Knicker-bocker reflects on the weeks after birthing her child:

> One day I read an article in the *Washington Post* about parents who accidentally left their babies in hot cars to die, because they forgot the baby was in the car seat in the back, sleeping. I stayed up all night in the bathroom, crying until I threw up. It happened over and over: a piece on the mothers and children of the Holocaust; a podcast about a woman, a survivor of Pol Pot's regime, taken to the Killing Fields with her two children. Every hour some atrocity, flying up out of history to remind me that the world was an open wound; turning me into each mother, my own son into each baby. Even though it wasn't happening to me, right this moment, it was happening to someone; it had happened and would happen. I had always known this, of course, but now I understood it. I felt it in my body—what had once been a sort of empathetic concern that I could turn on and off, or at least push away for a while, had become an inescapable physical state.[5]

But, Knickerbocker writes, this physical state eventually leaves her:

> Eventually, the excess of empathy I was suffering from started to wear off, like an old spell. I stopped crying all night on the bathroom floor. I started sleeping. I grew a skin again, that barrier between oneself and the world that is

necessary for survival. Was there something I could have done to fix myself faster? I would love to say that I took action, that I had some kind of agency. But I just waited. It didn't seem as if I had any other choice. It was something beyond me, outside of my control. It was a fog; it lifted.[6]

Courtney Martin, blogging for *On Being*, describes her experience with postpartum anxiety similarly, as a kind of temporary state:

> Over time, the vigilance waned. I imagine it like the smallest, most gradual leak in the tire of a bicycle. And the truth is, when I'm lying in bed and I hear the sound of one of my children (I now have two—ages four and one) gasp for breath with croup or gag as if to throw up, my body fills with that familiar anxiety instantaneously. But it ebbs and flows. I am learning that to be a mother is to know that you can't know everything will be okay and still operate as if you could. The alternative is to have your entire body—heart, mind, and soul—be held hostage by fear.[7]

I wonder whether we as black parents inhabit a different reality. For us, does this anxious vigilance, the fear for our own children and others' that Knickerbocker describes as an "excess of empathy," eventually fade away? I don't want to be held hostage by fear, but I'm not sure how to avoid that. It feels as if there's some ancestral knowledge deep in my bones driving my desire to keep a protective bubble around my daughter for as long as I can. In an essay about her son's birth, Jesmyn

Ward consults the historical record and offers an account of the violent and purposeful destruction of black families during slavery. She writes:

> One day, I read about an enslaved woman whose master was working her to death to pick as much cotton as she could on a plantation in Mississippi. She was pregnant and bore a child. During the day, she left her child at the edge of the cotton field where others would watch it, so she could toil down the rows. She had no choice. Her child cried, and it distracted her, slowed the accumulation of cotton bolls in her sack. The overseer noticed. He told her to mind her row, not her child. Still, it was as if she was sensitive to the keening of the baby. She tried to ignore her child's cries and focus on the rows, but still she lagged. The overseer warned her again. The enslaved woman tried to silence her tender mother's heart, but couldn't; her infant's cries muddled her movements, bound her fingers. The overseer noticed for the last time, and in a fit of rage he stalked to the infant crying for milk at the edge of the field and killed it. In the overseer's estimation, the mother was a machine—a wagon, perhaps, made to bear and transport loads. The child: a broken wheel. Something to remove to make the wagon serviceable again. After I read this, I couldn't help but imagine the woman, speechless and broken. Dragging her way through the American fields.[8]

This hits me harder than a devastating true story from the Holocaust or from the Cambodian Killing Fields might. This is a true story that connects to our family's lineage as black Americans, the descendants of slaves. I read this passage once, quickly, and then not again until I write this. I have to titrate my exposure. As my eyes scan the words, my stomach surges. How did that woman survive? Did she *want* to survive in the wake of such a barbaric act? How much has changed really, and how do the mothers of children killed by the state, her contemporary counterparts, survive? On the day I write this, Attorney General Jeff Sessions gives a speech to the National Sheriffs' Association in which he says, "The office of sheriff is a critical part of the Anglo-American heritage of law enforcement. We must never erode this historic office."[9] From overseer to officer, as rapper KRS-One put it.

Though I've given it some thought in the wake of the 2016 election, it doesn't seem there is any place to run to that will be safe for a black girl child and me, given the global trend toward xenophobic authoritarian regimes and the doubling down of patriarchal forces. I'm not sure where to flee or what to do with my fear, so I have carved up the question "How do we survive?" into something very small and manageable, a question that I do my best to answer at my kitchen table, at the stove, at the sink, on the floor in my daughter's room, in my bed where I nurse her, in the bathroom where I sit with her and coax her to tinkle on the potty, tell her she's not really washing her hands if she's not rubbing them together. There is a parenting podcast I listen to in part because the name is so good: *The Longest Shortest Time*. I've heard it said by more experienced parents that the phrase accurately describes parenting young children. The days drag on, but the years fly by.

I am digging into this longest shortest time in an effort to savor every moment.

As my daughter gets older—as she enters preschool and then kindergarten and beyond—I expect that my attention will be pulled again to the outside world. I expect that the Important Topics Discussed by Important People, the public conversations, will interest me, and eventually the two of us will talk them through together. But for now, I value slow and deliberate action in this domestic sphere above all else. I am committed to caring for Is, caring for myself, and seeing whether we can together be the change we want to see in the world.

Figuring out how I feel about discipline gives me an early opportunity. My daughter is leaving marks—nicks from her fingernails, impressions from her teeth—across my body. She bites my leg hard through my jeans while I'm cooking because I can't pick her up just then. She swipes at my face because I don't immediately scramble to read to her after she shouts, "Booh! Booh!" and points at the bookshelf. Sometimes she just bruises my ego. She kicks me hard in the stomach while I'm trying to change her diaper.

When I ask, "Why would you hurt Mama? Does Mama hurt you?" she responds, "No . . . no . . .," with a look of serious concern, and then goes right back to rapid-fire kicking and squealing with laughter. She goes in for a kiss, and I squeeze her in anticipation just before she sinks her six teeth into my cheek.

She is eighteen months old, and I understand that she comprehends much more than she can verbalize. I understand that she is frustrated and wants attention by any means necessary. I understand this is all developmentally appropriate. But it's also annoying, and sometimes it's dangerous. Sometimes it drains what I feel might be the last bit of energy that's keeping me upright and lucid enough to care for her. She seems to pull it together mostly when we're out of the house and in public spaces, but in the privacy of our home I am that mother one might look at pityingly and think, "How can she let that child run her like that?" Her dad and I have decided not to reprimand her physically. No spanking or, if you prefer, no popping her on the hand or swatting her legs. We use so many euphemisms for what is really just hitting a child, using violence to teach them violence is wrong.

I was spanked occasionally as a kid and it was fine. I don't have any scary memories about the spankings. I don't feel traumatized. I was never hit by a man or by anyone who regularly used their size or strength to intimidate me. I was spanked only by my mom, who was petite and pretty even-keeled emotionally. She did it hard enough to hurt but halfheartedly just the same, as if I'd left her no other option and she was sad about that. I only ever remember being spanked on my butt or my thighs, places with enough meat to absorb the impact of her hand or the belt. She didn't scream while she spanked me, and she certainly didn't call me names, either then or any other time. I have talked to friends who were spanked as kids and who now call it abuse, and usually one of these things that never happened to me was happening to them. They were hit in the face, or they were hit with things like house shoes or extension cords.

So if there is a way to employ a kinder, gentler approach to spanking, I know it and could use my own experience to guide how I reprimand my daughter for serious infractions. Still, I choose to use the word "violence" to describe the use of physical discipline, though it feels a little dramatic. As a black mother, framing it in this way is a political choice. It's a reminder that I want my daughter to know that her body is her own, that pain at others' hands is not a natural part of life, and that no authority figure—whether it's me now or some teacher or police officer later in her life—has the right to hurt her as a way to force obedience.

❧

I'M NOT ALONE IN WANTING MY HOME TO BE A MICROCOSM of the world I want to live in. Kim Tabari, a mother in Southern California, is active in the Long Beach chapter of Black Lives Matter and cofounded a social justice group for children that includes her eleven-year-old son. "It wouldn't make sense for me to carry out some kind of violence at my house and then want to stand up for people who have been attacked in the street," she tells me. I hear this refusal to perpetuate violence in the home from other mothers engaged in political work. "We can't do to our kids what white people have done to our kids and our people," says Jessica Black, who works with the Black Organizing Project in the San Francisco Bay Area and is mother to a thirteen-year-old daughter and nineteen-year-old son. When she became a mom at nineteen, she used the discipline tactics she'd grown up with, which centered on whuppings and yelling. But when her son was around five or six, her own political consciousness was developing, and her thinking on discipline changed. She turned to talking through behavioral problems with him instead, and she's used the same approach with her daughter. Black has faced judgment from family members, who have said that her children talk back and need whuppings. "They're not talking back," Black says. "They're learning how to articulate themselves. They have lots of opinions, which is not the way that I came up, not the way that my mom and aunts came up." She worries that if she instills fear in her children through physical discipline, they will be afraid in situations where she wants them to be confident and strong willed, like with educators Black's family views as hostile. "My daughter couldn't stand up for herself in school if I was beating on her all the time."

For Trina Greene Brown, founder of a support community for black parents called Parenting for Liberation, mutual accountability figures into her approach to rule setting and discipline. Greene Brown's work to end gender-based violence routinely puts her in meetings with others building and sustaining social justice movements. She noticed that any training or workshop she was in always started with establishing community agreements. Members of a group agree on the norms they'll use to conduct themselves, and anyone can suggest an addition to the list. Participants buy in on the front end, making it hard for anyone to later claim she was being held to a standard she didn't accept. Greene Brown's eight-year-old son had complained that it was unfair that she made all the rules without any input from him. Now he can request certain types of behavior of her as well. A recent ask was that she not raise her voice with him as much. They're flattening a hierarchy her son didn't want to live under and she didn't want to impose. Greene Brown's politics pointed a way toward how to address power imbalances—perceived and real—within her family. "These conversations around my accountability to him wouldn't exist if I wasn't working really hard on ensuring that there's accountability to black folks," she tells me. "I'm trying to ask people to be accountable to me, and here I am not trying to be accountable to my own son."

With our commitment to adopting nonphysical approaches to discipline, Greene Brown, Black, Tabari, and I are moving against the cultural current. In her groundbreaking book, *Spare the Kids: Why Whupping Children Won't Save Black America*, journalist and children's advocate Stacey Patton details how an authoritarian approach to black parenting developed in the first place and why spanking is common in our communities. These beatings were born of a fear that if, as a black parent, you did not go to great lengths to teach your child his or her place, then some white person would someday do so with much more violence and far more serious consequences. The violence inflicted by black parents on their children was born out of both love and a deep, abiding fear for that child's ability to survive the American caste system that devalues black life. And while some may associate the need for such tough love with the conditions of slavery or the Jim Crow era, many black families understand that that caste system and the risks inherent to it survive to this day.

But not all black mothers with critiques of how authority functions in the wider world use democratic methods at home. Cat Brooks is an Oakland-based black liberation movement leader and cofounder of the Anti-Police Terror Project, an organization that supports the families of people killed or violated by police. Given what she knows about the ever-present possibility of state violence, Brooks has relied on more traditional forms of discipline to keep her twelve-year-old daughter safe. "I'm worried about her life, literally. I'm worried about her survival," Brooks tells me. "Structure and discipline are important. There's not horizontal decision making in my household." Brooks mostly uses what she calls "the fear of God" rather than physical discipline with her daughter. "I don't know that screaming or threatening is better, but she's clear that I will put hands on her if I have to."

Greene Brown of Parenting for Liberation told me some black parents she speaks to are incredulous when she encourages them to abandon more aggressive techniques. "I've gone into communities where I've gotten pushback," she says. "'No, we have to beat our kids! What are you talking about? If I don't do XYZ, then they're gonna be in a gang!' What can I say to that parent?" That line of thinking—that a black child raised too leniently will end up dead or in jail—is reinforced in pop culture. In his latest comedy special, *Tamborine*, Chris Rock does a bit on parenting: "If you don't punch your black son in the face, that's child abuse . . . It's important that your black son follow your instructions. It's the difference between life and death," he told a Brooklyn audience in 2017. This tough love approach meant to make the boundaries in a child's world crystal clear shows up again later in his routine: "I tell my kids: 'Outside this house, no one gives a fuck about you. No one thinks you're cute. No one wants to hear your opinion.'" The crowd laughs with recognition.

But this strict, unyielding approach to parenting can have unintended consequences, says Aya de Leon, a scholar and writer in Berkeley who is mother to a nine-year-old girl. She says she's encountered the type of parents Greene Brown mentions, the type who think a rule-by-fear approach will keep their kids safe. When these same kids actually *do* end up in gangs or in dangerous relationships with domineering men, the parents wonder how this could have happened. "I didn't raise them like that" is a common refrain. "Well, in some ways you did," de Leon says. "You raised them to respect authoritarian structures."

In her book *Spare the Kids*, Patton is aware of the fine line she walks in calling out adults in black families, who are already so maligned. First, she points out that because the institution of slavery kept normal family relations out of reach for black Americans, it has only been in the last 150 years that we have been allowed to legally parent our children. It makes some sense that we are disproportionately reliant on violent means of establishing control when the threat of violence hung over our ancestors' lives for the past 400 years. We've also had a relatively short amount of time to practice something else. Patton takes on potential criticism directly, writing that while she is aware of stereotypes that blame black parenting, and specifically black mothering, as the source of society's ills, "the deification of black mothers is just as damaging as white racist stereotypes against them. . . . We put Mama on a pedestal and hesitate to call her out because she's holding up our families, often by herself. But that doesn't make it OK for her to beat the black off us."

She's right. We should acknowledge damage done at the hands of some black mothers. One conversation in particular reminds me that many grown-ups are still suffering because of physical punishments they received as kids. In June 2017, I make my annual pilgrimage to Detroit for the Allied Media Conference, a convening of activists, artists, and media makers I've been a part of for more than a decade. I mention to some black women who are also longtime participants that I'm working on a project on black mothering and am surprised when several of them immediately want to talk about the beatings they themselves endured as children at the hands of their own mothers.

Tawana Petty is a forty-year-old Detroit-based writer and mother to a twenty-one-year-old son. "I was raised 'spare the rod, spoil the child,'" she tells me. Then she uses a word that will stay lodged in my mind whenever I think about the stories I've heard since childhood about whuppings, stories that involve belts or switches from trees. "My mom would go get a weapon," Petty says, adding that she was often frightened of her mother when she was angry. She remembers changing grades to avoid getting a beating, but those poor grades were a result of what was going on at home. She now has a better understanding of what may have motivated her mother's behavior. The woman had been sixteen at the time of Petty's birth, and her own mother died just three months later. "It is nearly impossible to know how to nurture a daughter when you weren't nurtured as a young girl yourself," Petty says. With her own son, she has tried to break the intergenerational cycle of violence. I ask how she did it. "A little bit of patience goes a long way," she says. "I had to make a commitment to not discipline him when I was at my highest level of anger."

Petty tells me that she made a critical departure from her earlier understandings of how the parent-child bond worked. "We're taught they don't become fully human until they're out on their own, and until then we own them. I tried not to replicate that. I needed my son to know that I recognize his humanity."

Parenting from a place of ownership can drive us toward a physically abusive approach to parenting. It can also cause us to be so overprotective that we smother our children. Tabari tells me she made a conscious decision not to smother eleven-year-old Azaan after witnessing the behavior of a friend, a mother of a teenaged black boy. After the teenager got into a fight on a bus in Long Beach, his mother forbade him from taking public transit, opting instead to drive him everywhere herself and otherwise curbing his independence. "She completely sheltered him because she was afraid. I said I'm not going to be that person," Tabari tells me. "I don't want to live with that kind of fear, which is why I do Kids for Freedom and Justice. I want to be in the habit of teaching him, of being joyful with him, exploring things, going places. Azaan has to know that whatever he learns at home he can take it with him. And I trust him to make the right decisions."

When I ask Tabari what she does, in addition to organizing the multiracial progressive political group for Azaan and other children, to keep her own fears at bay, she says she orients toward joy. "I try to have fun with him. We try to laugh a lot. Be silly. I try to remember that he's a little boy. You know how people are always like, 'How's the little man?' I'm like, 'He's not a man, he's a boy.' We love calling them 'little man,' but he's a boy."

By insisting that others see her son as the child he is, Tabari is taking a stand in the face of the larger society's frequent failure to see black children as children. Whether it's twelve-year-old Tamir Rice in a Cleveland playground with a toy gun or seventeen-year-old Trayvon Martin walking home with his Skittles and iced tea, black children who have been victims of police or vigilante violence are often denied the presumption of innocence. These skewed perceptions can result in tragic deaths or in unnecessarily harsh discipline at school. A recent study found that white women undergraduates perceive black boys as young as ten to be four to five years older than they are.[10]

I want to give my daughter room to act out, to be a toddler who doesn't yet know how to effectively express her emotions. I even want to give her room to experiment publicly with bad behavior and learn for herself what it takes to get the response she wants. But I'm also terrified of being too lenient and thereby abdicating my responsibility to keep her safe and to prepare her for a world that will deny her the messy missteps of childhood that white children are allowed. Like the mothers I speak with, Patton's book suggests alternatives to spanking: denying privileges, taking away screen time and electronics, giving extra chores, talking through the issue at hand—all things that take time, patience, and finely honed communication skills on the parent's part. It's a lot harder than simply letting one's instincts take over. Every time my daughter catches me off guard with a bite or a scratch, I override the urge to grab her wrist or swat her bottom. I think back to what Petty tells me about never disciplining her son when she was at the height of her anger. I don't want to discipline Is when I'm at the height of my frustration or exhaustion. Still, I'm not exactly sure what to do. I can't reason with her yet. What nonviolent discipline techniques can I use with a child this young?

LisaGay Hamilton is an actor living in Los Angeles. Her sons are fifteen and seven. She tells me my instincts are right when I swiftly place my daughter in the Pack N' Play I keep in the kitchen as punishment for her biting, scratching, and tantrums. I firmly tell her no; then I put her in the mesh cage and let her wail while I go on about my business, cooking or washing dishes or doing whatever else I'm up to. Most importantly, I turn my attention away from her. "It's a time out. It's the separating," Hamilton tells me, sharing what still works with her younger child. "For Sekou, anytime you say, 'Go to your room,' it's 'No, no, no!' We live in the kitchen. And the idea of leaving the core and being upstairs by yourself is an issue."

Today the Pack N' Play works. Who knows what we'll come up with for the next stage in her development. I do know I want to stay this course. I'm inspired by A. Rochaun Meadows-Fernandez's words in her piece "After

Charlottesville: We Need to Start 'Spoiling' Our Black Children."[11] She writes, "We owe it to ourselves and our children to hold them as tight as we can. We may be the only ones to ever do so." It's only a matter of time before too many of my daughter's actions are misinterpreted as dangerous or defiant just because she's a black girl. Someday soon enough she'll be reprimanded harshly by someone who doesn't recognize her fierce and courageous spirit for what it is. When that happens, I'm hoping she'll be able to recover relatively easily, resourcing herself with memories of the nurturing she received at home even through the tantrums of her terrible twos.

CHAPTER 3

Family

I AM THE DAUGHTER OF AN UNMARRIED BLACK WOMAN. I AM NOW AN unmarried black woman raising a girl. I didn't grow up with my father at home. As has been the case since soon after her first birthday, my daughter isn't either.

I didn't meet my father until I was in my early twenties. Our meeting was healing and answered questions that had been roaming around my mind for years, like who he was and why he'd been away. But his absence hadn't mattered in the ways some people assumed it should. I grew up in a house in the suburbs, the same house where my mom and her sisters and their dad before them had grown up. My maternal grandmother had grown up around the corner. We had a big in-ground pool in the backyard where I'd swim with my cousins and other neighborhood kids. I grew up playing soccer and riding horses and skiing, and on the few occasions that I was referred to jokingly as a Cosby kid, I knew what that meant. I was privileged, maybe even a little spoiled. As an only child, I was the focus of my mom's attention and resources. That investment in my success and happiness was supplemented by the love, time, and money of other adults in our family, especially by my maternal aunt, Pam, who lived with my mom and me from the time I was seven. Extended family was everything, and while the word "family" seemed to mean a mom and dad and siblings to some, to me it's always meant aunts and uncles and cousins and grandparents and the neighborhood elders who watched you grow up. I always had a kind of unvarnished pride in my upbringing. None of the weird assumptions people seemed to have about "single mothers" applied to my life.

And yet that condemnation of single parents is what we hear again and again from politicians, pundits, and some academics. On Father's Day in 2008, candidate Obama reminded a predominately black congregation in Chicago about the importance of having a father in the home. "Children who grow up without a father are five times more likely to live in poverty and commit crime; nine times more likely to drop out of schools and twenty times more likely to end up in prison," he said, suggesting that two-parent families are a kind of talisman capable of protecting children from tough lives.[1]

During a 2012 presidential debate, Mitt Romney, upon being asked by CNN's Candy Crawley how to combat gun violence, replied in part:

> We need moms and dads helping raise kids . . . To tell our kids that before they have babies, they ought to think about getting married to someone—that's a great idea because if there's a two-parent family, the prospect of living in poverty

goes down dramatically. The opportunities that the child will . . . be able to achieve increase dramatically. So we can make changes in the way our culture works to help bring people away from violence and give them opportunity and bring them in the American system.[2]

From both Democrats and Republicans, liberals and conservatives, the message for years has been that those of us who don't marry before we have kids are somehow outside, as Romney put it in those 2012 remarks, the "American system." When some public figure starts railing against the horrors of unmarried women having babies, class is the primary issue, even if they don't acknowledge it.

For context, some numbers: In 2015, 40 percent of black, female-headed households with children lived in poverty. For white families headed by an unmarried woman, 30.6 percent lived in poverty.[3] As a black child and now as a black mother, my household was and is among that 60 percent majority that's above the poverty line. I worry about what's lost when we don't talk about how that 60 percent is often doing just fine or why that 40 percent is actually impoverished. Not being married may correlate with being poor, but it doesn't cause it.

Like me, my daughter is growing up without a dad at home, but the similarities in our experiences end there. My father lived across the country—he'd moved west before I was born to pursue a graduate degree—and we had no contact until I sought him out and initiated a conversation that led to us staying in touch for a few years. My daughter's dad also lives in a different city, but he was by my side during her birth and cared for her daily during the first year of her life while we were still together romantically and before he left town for a job. He visits her often and video chats with her daily, and they have a relationship that I support and that brings us all a lot of joy.

It's not easy, but we work at it. For about six months after our breakup, we were in therapy to learn how to be on this coparenting journey together. I'm proud of us when I read a line from a 2008 study: "We conclude that parents' ability to work together in rearing their common child across households helps keep nonresident fathers connected to their children and that programs aimed at improving parents' ability to communicate may have benefits for children irrespective of whether the parents' romantic relationship remains intact."[4] We created our own program with the coaching of a black woman who talked us through some ugly, painful periods and helped us put our goals and commitments on paper. Now here we are—making the road by walking.

My father and my daughter's father are college-educated black men from middle-class families. They both grew up with their dads at home. At the time of their children's births, they were gainfully employed or training to advance in a profession. They were not ripped away by death or by the criminal justice system or by the pull of the Streets™. They just happened to be in relationships that produced children but didn't work out. I've never understood why this phenomenon is so troubling to the ubiquitous marriage promoters. I've never understood why we celebrate an institution's ability to maintain itself in part by making it expensive and stigmatizing to leave unhappy unions. None of this is to disparage marriage. There must be something magical and transformative about giving your life a structure and deciding that you and another person will work within that, no matter what. But those of us who opt for other structures with which to organize our lives shouldn't be shamed when we have children.

There's nothing tragic about the circumstances that have kept myself and my daughter from growing up in the same house as our fathers. Our stories have to do with romantic relationships that didn't last and being born in a somewhat bland midwestern city that ambitious black folks are often eager to leave in favor of big-city job opportunities and culture. Not all black single moms have such a benign family backstory. For every one hundred black women in communities around the country, there are just eighty-three black men. "The remaining men—1.5 million of them—are, in a sense, missing," the New York Times reported in April 2015, and incarceration and early death are to blame.[5] There's no comparable gender gap for white people. The article revealed that for every one hundred white women, there are ninety-nine white men. But nearly one in twelve black men between the ages of twenty-five and fifty-four are behind bars, a rate that's five times that of nonblack men that age. The imbalance between free, alive black boys and free, alive black girls starts during the teen years and peaks in the thirties. (To be clear, black women are disproportionately incarcerated, too: one in two hundred black women are behind bars, compared to one in five hundred nonblack women.) These data help clarify why 30 percent of black families are headed by unmarried women, compared to 13 percent of American households overall.[6] And how do unpartnered black women feel about their predicament? According to the *Times* analysis, "The black women left behind find that potential partners of the same race are scarce, while men, who face an abundant supply of potential mates, don't need to compete as hard to find one." Commenting on the findings and his own research, University of Chicago economist Kerwin Charles told the *Times* that "men seem less likely to commit to romantic relationships, or to work hard to maintain them."

In other words, black men are often unavailable for family life on two fronts—one group caught up in the carceral net, the other so puffed up or freaked out by their endangered-species status that they can't be bothered to settle down, at least not with black women. I'm eager to get the read of someone with a bird's-eye view of these issues. G. Rosaline Preudhomme is a seventy-three-year-old grandmother and organizer in Washington, DC. Her outreach to black communities is credited with helping pass the city's Initiative 71, which legalized marijuana. Preudhomme's work seeks to address the systemic reason for these "missing" black men. To her, the so-called war on drugs has targeted young black men for using and selling drugs, while others who use and sell are simply not policed or prosecuted as heavily. She says that harsh drug policies have kept black men from community life even postincarceration by restricting where people with criminal records can live, go to school, and work. "It's the resilient spirit of black women that has gotten us through these past four hundred years of our family life always being disrupted," Preudhomme says when we talk.

Fifty thousand people were behind bars for nonviolent drug offenses in 1980. By 1997, that number had jumped to more than four hundred thousand, close to where it remains to this day.[7] Despite the tremendous pressure punitive drug policies have put on black communities in the past forty years, our families persist. That's in part because black Americans have had a structure for organizing family life that predates the drug war and accommodates the absence or intermittent presence of parents.

We've had to. Prior to emancipation, slave owners routinely destabilized enslaved people's lives, keeping them from maintaining kinship structures rooted in blood ties. Marriages and parent-child relationships meant little in the face of the institution's drive for profit. In her 1971 essay, "Reflections on the Black Woman's Role in the Community of Slaves," Angela Davis wrote, "The American brand of slavery strove toward a rigidified disorganization in family life ... Mothers and fathers were brutally separated; children, when they became of age, were branded and frequently severed from their mothers." Family as a concept became elastic and inclusive as enslaved people maintained human connections despite slave owners' frequent severing of bonds. Scholars have pointed out that collective child-rearing practices were a feature of many precolonial African societies, and so African descendants had a model for how to create networks of care that didn't depend on biological relationship.[8]

In 1974, a young white anthropologist named Carol Stack published *All Our Kin*, about her three years living among families in a poor, black section of an unnamed midwestern city.

The book is her exploration of the strategies these families used to cope with poverty, but much of what she reports is familiar to me as someone who grew up in the 1980s and 1990s in a middle-class family. The notion of "illegitimacy" wasn't really a thing or, as Stack puts it, "a child's existence seems to legitimize the child in the eyes of the community." Adult women, either sharing a home or supporting each other across households, formed kinship networks as a way to take care of themselves and their children. Even census statistics on female-headed households were misleading since, as Stack found, these families commonly consisted of three generations of kin under one roof, and so children were in the care of multiple adults even if the mother was "single" to an outsider's eyes.[9]

The takeaway from Stack's study is that low-income black women stayed unmarried not because they were emotionally broken or too promiscuous to commit or besieged by some other moral failing. They weren't marrying because they had faith that their aunts and cousins and mothers and friends—with the help of their low-wage jobs and welfare benefits—would be better able to help them and their children survive than would a man with dubious job prospects. These women weren't cynically underestimating a potential partner's earning power. Stack found that they were instead taking a clear-eyed look at how black people fared under American capitalism, seeing that the game was rigged and opting for the safer bet. Her book concluded: "Distinctively negative features attributed to poor families, that they are fatherless, matrifocal, unstable, and disorganized, are not general characteristics of black families living substantially below economic subsistence in urban America. The black urban family, embedded in cooperative domestic exchange, proves to be an organized tenacious, active, lifelong network."[10]

In taking this village-oriented approach to child-rearing, black Americans may be out of step with mainstream white, middle-class American culture, which became more centered on the nuclear family at the middle of the last century with the advent of mass suburbanization. But we're fully in step with how the rest of the world has functioned throughout most of history. A body of research has determined that Western, educated, industrialized, rich, democratic (or WEIRD) countries, with their focus on the nuclear family, bring up children in what anthropologist David Lancy has called "a departure from all other human culture."[11] Most humans across time and space are "cooperative breeders" and depend on adult women and older children in the extended family and community to care for the young. When I talk about caring for my daughter, I talk about how "we" are raising her. I might say, "We don't spank her as a form of discipline," or "We just started potty training." I'm not referring exclusively to my daughter's dad and myself when I use this language. Instead, I mean him, my mom, his mom, his sister, my aunt when she can help out, and the young black women we pay for childcare—the people who are in the innermost circle of caring for my daughter.

Those of us who are organizing our families outside of the structure of marriage are both replicating long-standing models and freestyling as we envision something new. In 2017 Lake Research Partners surveyed 379 women nationwide who are not married and who have children under eighteen at home.[12]

Black and Latina women were oversampled. When asked who played a major role in raising their children, the women said they're most helped by someone in their immediate family, their children's father, their current partner, members of their children's father's family, and their children's siblings. The vast majority of the 253 married women included in the same survey said their spouse plays the biggest supporting role in child-rearing.

∂♥

ZAHRA ALABANZA LIKES TO SAY THAT SHE INHERITED her sons. When she was twenty-nine, she learned that her nephews, ages one and four, were in foster care in another state. At the time, Alabanza had all the trappings of a successful young professional's life. She had just bought a condo in Chicago, and she had a master's degree and a full-time job. In addition to having the financial means to care for the boys, she had the emotional and political framework to understand how significant her presence could be for their lives. She had spent time in foster care herself, and her career was in social work. She knew that once in the child welfare system, older black children rarely get out. She was also at an age where she could feel her body craving motherhood, she tells me. As she sees it now, "I manifested my boys."

In the nine years since starting life with her sons, Alabanza has been on a quest to define what family looks like for them. She refers to the two people who have the most stable and consistent presence in her sons' lives as her "baby mommas." Unlike me, she doesn't have a network of blood family to rely on, so she's creating kinship in other ways. She lists people in New York, New Orleans, and Chicago who visit for long stretches or to whom the boys travel. There's family in Atlanta as well: A former romantic partner is still in their lives in meaningful ways, supporting her when she's bending under the weight of parenting and holding the boys accountable when they act out. Another friend keeps the boys overnight midweek.

As she's built community for her sons, Alabanza has found the hardest part to be defining each person's role. Earlier in her parenting journey, it felt important to have someone she could call a coparent. There have been five people she's referred to as such, only one of whom was a romantic partner and none of whom contributed financially. But sometimes these people didn't show up like she'd needed them to. Now she's focused on creating the consistency and commitment she hasn't always known how to lock in, which means being explicit about what she and the boys need. Moving away from seeking a coparent has also meant confronting her desire to mirror nuclear family traditions and find one person she could rely on to help carry the load.

"It took a long time to realize that I could reconfigure it a different way," she tells me. She thinks the nuclear family can be too isolating, cutting mothers off not only from help but also from the kind of useful meddling that can alert us when we're in bad situations. "Think about the homegirl who got married, had kids, and moved to the suburbs, who you see once a month. You don't know what's going on in that household. Then she's calling you to come help her move."

It's true that marriage acts as a kind of shield against scrutiny, while being unmarried with children invites all kinds of negative assumptions. If you're married, you and your children must be thriving. If you're a so-called single mom, things must be a mess. Alabanza's life challenges these beliefs, and her approach to romance adds another layer to her quest to create family. She identifies as queer and polyamorous, meaning that she's open to multiple romantic relationships simultaneously. Just as she ideally would like to receive love from a number of sources, she wants that for her sons, too. There's nothing newfangled about this; black kinship networks have always functioned this way. "The extended family was the queerness of the family," Alabanza tells me.

It may be off-putting to some to describe as "queer" a family within which there's no same-sex partnering, but I'm beginning to embrace this description. Even when they're composed of people who identify as straight, black families often challenge heteronormative ideas of family. It's time we proudly name the specific ways that what Alabanza calls "the queerness of the family" can benefit those of us involved. In her essay "Man Child," black feminist thinker Audre Lorde writes about raising her son in a lesbian household and how her partnership upended traditional ideas of power. Her son was nearly four when Lorde and her partner met. At the time of her writing, he is fourteen. She writes:

> Jonathan has had the advantage of growing up within a nonsexist relationship, one in which this society's pseudo-natural assumptions of ruler/ruled are being

challenged. And this is not only because Frances and I are lesbians, for unfortunately there are some lesbians who are still locked into patriarchal patterns of unequal power relationships. These assumptions of power relationships are being questioned because Frances and I, often painfully and with varying degrees of success, attempt to evaluate and measure over and over again our feelings concerning power, our own and others'. . . . Most importantly, as the son of lesbians, he has had an invaluable model—not only of relationship but of relating.[13]

Elsewhere in the essay, Lorde writes about the importance of reassessing power "as something other than might, age, privilege or the lack of fear."[14] I think about my own childhood growing up with my mom and my maternal aunt. The first words that come to mind are "calm" and "even-keeled." In the decade before I left home for college, when the three of us lived together, I can remember only one or two times there were raised voices or emotionally fraught heavy silences. This is not to say that only men struggle with their tempers. But men are more often socialized to believe that explosive anger and a pouty retreat into themselves are appropriate ways to communicate. I grew up never threatened with "wait till your father gets home," never seeing one adult's needs prioritized over another's. I saw two adults treating each other with love, respect, and humor. I saw that it was possible to be a whole, healthy adult without marriage and, in my aunt's case, without biological children of one's own. Throughout my thirties, I was sympathetic but somewhat baffled as I watched some women friends struggle to make peace with their unmarried, unpartnered status. Many of them seemed to feel that kids were unlikely since no partner was in sight, but their predicaments just looked to me like another way to do life. Because of my own upbringing, I felt liberated from the assumption that marriage and mothering must go together. Mainstream culture's glorification of marriage leaves so many people feeling unnecessarily deflated and out of options when that type of union doesn't materialize.

I feel a swell of recognition when on Father's Day 2018 I see black feminist writer Amber J. Phillips tweeting about her own father: "Because he opted out of being [a] parent, I was raised with the radical idea that I don't actually need a patriarch in my home or life to be happy or feel a false sense of success."[15] In her 1987 essay "The Meaning of Motherhood in Black Culture and Black Mother/Daughter Relationships," Patricia Hill Collins writes that growing up in a household like mine (and presumably like Phillips's) in which working mothers and extended family support are common creates a kind of domino effect. Generation after generation, black women reject ideas that patriarchal family—and, by extension, patriarchy in the broader society—is normal. Instead, black girls grow up with a sense of empowerment and possibility that girls of other races don't necessarily see modeled at home or in their communities. "Since Black mothers have a distinctive relationship to white patriarchy, they may be less likely to socialize their daughters into their proscribed roles as subordinates," Collins writes.[16]

I think we've underestimated how powerful this is. Black families have created a container for passing on to our

children a culture that repels the forces of white supremacy and creates ample opportunities to question patriarchy.
But our reliance on extended family networks and collective
approaches to childcare, our rejection of the nuclear family
as the only way to organize our lives, has been consistently
derided throughout history. The safety zones that black parents have created, with leadership from black mothers, the
places where we learn that we are not who the world tells us
we are, have been criticized by everyone from Daniel Patrick
Moynihan in the 1960s to the American Enterprise Institute's W. Bradford Wilcox today. People such as these, with
assists from others across the political spectrum, argue that
we have too many female-headed households, too few legal
marriages, and that black mothers are, as Michele Wallace
put it in her groundbreaking 1978 book, *Black Macho and the
Myth of the Superwoman*, "too strong, too hard, too evil, too
castrating." Moynihan's 1965 Department of Labor report
argued, as Wallace paraphrases, that "this abnormal family
structure made it nearly impossible for blacks to benefit from
and participate in the American power structure. And the
primary feature of this abnormality was the 'matriarch,' the
'strong black woman.'"[17]

It makes sense that black women's reproductive decisions—
not just our efforts to avoid childbearing but also our efforts
to parent in ways that diverge from the mainstream—
are policed so heavily. Mothers transmit culture. When we
transmit a culture that reinforces the idea that the emperor
has no clothes, that's a problem for the emperor and everyone participating in the mass delusion that keeps him on

the throne. Our truth telling, our lack of practice genu-
flecting to illegitimate power, is especially significant today,
with someone intent on portraying himself as the ultimate
strong-man patriarch occupying the White House. Suddenly
"the American power structure" Moynihan wrote about decades ago looks like less and less of a good thing to more and
more people. Who better to lead as we imagine and create
alternatives to patriarchy than those who never fit in the
old system?

But unmarried black mothers and their daughters aren't
lauded for holding the keys to resisting patriarchal oppression.
Instead, the dominant narrative is that we're poor, draining
public coffers, and so a blight on society.[18] Some academics,
politicians, and pundits seem certain of the link between
poverty and remaining unmarried. But I would argue that
economically stable, educated individuals tend to marry each
other. They stay out of poverty because they weren't impoverished in the first place. The marriage promoters want us to
believe that getting married will automatically lift poor people
out of poverty. But if you're from and have stayed in a low-
income community, your peers and potential mates are most
likely also low-income. Poor plus poor does not somehow
equal middle class. It means two poor adults raising poor kids
and trying to figure out how to survive. There's a reason that
the depressing adage "I can do bad all by myself" has been
written into the lines of black women characters in chitlin-
circuit shows since time immemorial.

I ask Mia Birdsong, a social policy fellow at New America, whether I'm missing something about the link between

marriage and poverty. "There's this idea that if you make people get married, then the men will feel some responsibility to provide for the mom and baby and get a job," she explains. But this line of thinking assumes that men aren't working because they're lazy and lack motivation, not because they can't find living wage work, Birdsong says. In other words, the marriage promotion rhetoric depends on a belief that black people have weak morals, not that we're challenged by entrenched structural barriers.

The storytelling that best illustrates why marriage promotion programs don't typically work in poor communities remains Katherine Boo's classic 2003 *New Yorker* article, "The Marriage Cure."[19] In it, Boo writes in rich detail about two black Oklahoma public housing residents and their families. Boo follows the women as they participate in a state-sponsored program at a local church that offers instruction on how to get and stay married. In the class, the male pastor tells the five women gathered that it's their job to convince reluctant men that marriage will improve their lives. The women share stories of past physical abuse at the hands of partners, of being demoralized by a partner's or father's abandonment, and of the stress of dating someone who's involved in violent crime. Boo writes that in this community "relationships with men were often what stopped an ambitious woman from escaping." Still, one of the women profiled, twenty-two-year-old Kim Henderson, is postponing having children and sees marriage as a key part of attaining what she calls "a healthy, wealthy, normal-lady life." Her best friend is Corean Brothers, who at forty-nine is divorced with five kids.

In one passage, Corean looks back at the marriage she left after her husband beat her:

> When she was eighteen, Corean left fruit-picking for the Job Corps, a Great Society program for the poor which had an opening in Oklahoma City. She became a certified nurse's aide. She also met a funny, conscientious man who worked on a loading dock. She did what the Holy Temple pastor was now recommending, and married. Over the years, she emptied bedpans in a nursing home and cleaned houses for the affluent, but her earnings—forty-five dollars a day for housekeeping—didn't cover day-care costs. Eventually, she became a stay-at-home mother. Then her husband, who had become a truck driver for Frito-Lay, declared bankruptcy. "Financially, he was struggling, and with the kids I could only take day work," Corean said. "He was angry at me for not pulling my weight, income-wise, while I believed the kids needed me at home. The fights just tore us apart."[20]

Romantic relationships are emotional endeavors and the business of those involved. Governments aren't equipped to understand all the pressures that low-income couples face. What governments *are* equipped to do is address poverty head on, by acknowledging and supporting people's economic and social rights. Instead, our government punishes unmarried mothers, sending the message that a husband can and should be a family's source of financial stability. Lost in the conversation connecting low marriage rates and poverty is the impact low-wage work has on black families. The question shouldn't be whether we can put together two measly paychecks but whether we as individuals can get paid a fair wage for the work that we do. You only have to look at how common black women's leadership has been in the recent fast-food workers' strikes demanding $15 per hour and the right to unionize to know that making work pay is another key to helping black families.

Such social policies as paid parental leave, universal childcare, and universal health care—common in other WEIRD countries—would also alleviate the financial pressures unmarried moms face. This kind of government intervention is why a single mother and her child in Denmark are no more likely to be poor than a married mother and her child.[21]

And yet we see how distressing this idea can be to some Americans, including mothers. Virginia Kruta, an associate editor at the conservative *Daily Caller*, expressed her dismay after attending a rally held by Cori Bush, a Democratic congressional candidate in St. Louis. The summer 2018 rally featured Alexandria Ocasio-Cortez, who had recently won a Democratic primary for a congressional seat representing parts of Queens and the Bronx. In her report, Kruta calls what she witnessed "truly terrifying," in part because she "saw how easy it would be, as a parent, to accept the idea that my children deserve healthcare and education."[22] These are progressive policies intended to lift all boats, and here's a conservative white woman offended by black (Bush) and Latina (Ocasio-Cortez) women declaring that the government should play a role in improving people's lives.

ঽৱ

BLACK MOTHERS HAVE ALWAYS WORKED. IN HER 1987
essay, "The Meaning of Motherhood in Black Culture and
Black Mother/Daughter Relationships," Collins explains
that slavery and the economic realities of Jim Crow made it
hard for black families to create the separate, gender-based
spheres of influence (father as economic provider and head of
household, mother as nurturer and subordinate) that white
America lauded as the ideal organization of family life. This
way of doing family was inaccessible but may have been foreign and undesirable to African descendants in the United
States regardless. The rigid segregation by sex of adults' roles
in a family was not a part of the West African tradition,
according to scholars, including Collins.[23]

I remember this bit of history when I read coverage of a
CDC study that corrects the misconception that black men
disproportionately abandon their children or otherwise shirk
their fatherly duties. Instead, black men are generally more
likely than men of other races to read to, feed, bathe, and play
with their young children on a regular basis, whether they live
in the same home as the child or not. The reliance on nonmarital birthrates to tell a story about parental involvement has
built a false narrative. Just because a father isn't married to his
child's mother doesn't mean he's an absent dad.[24]

Birdsong, the family policy analyst, thinks black men
don't get enough credit for sharing in the work of running
the home and raising the kids. "Middle-class white men are at
this place where they want to take paternity leave and share

household responsibilities and really lean into this space of not being their fathers," she tells me. "The message that black men get is that they have to reach for this 1950s standard of what a father is supposed to do. White dudes are trying to do what black men are already doing."

It's the summer of 2017, and I am thinking about all this in the context of a cartoon called "You Should've Asked" that's gone viral online.[25] It opens with the artist, Emma, recounting how she once visited a male colleague's house for dinner. When she gets there, his wife is cooking dinner for the adults and trying unsuccessfully to get their sullen children to eat theirs. The husband is on the couch, sipping a drink, talking, and entertaining the family's guest. Soon, dinner boils over and is ruined because the wife's attention has been pulled in too many directions. "What did you do?" the husband asks, annoyed and surprised. "Everything," the wife responds. "I did everything." The husband replies that his wife should've asked for help, and the rest of Emma's cartoon is an incisive illustration of what she calls "the mental load," the invisible and never-ending work that women, especially mothers, take on as domestic managers. Sure, their male partners may do some chores, but usually only because wifey saw the need and delegated the task. The seeing, remembering, and managing are themselves work, and too few men recognize it.

When I see the cartoon, my daughter's father and I are still together, and I recognize myself in the situations Emma draws. But I don't repost, because it's the kind of thing that opens the door to a million "not all men" comments, which I don't want to hear, especially not from my partner. I also don't share the cartoon because even though I can identify, it comes off as a white feminist complaint.

I have the same feeling when, a year later, writers Cheryl Strayed and Steve Almond take up the topic of invisible labor on their *Dear Sugars* podcast. As I listen to the letters of people who have written to Strayed and Almond seeking advice, I think, "Get out of your relationship. Don't accept a marriage in which you have to manage an adult partner like a child." But I know that most heterosexual women would rather figure out how to correct and lessen the harm of men's socialization than toss out relationships with them altogether. And I still know there won't be a chorus of black women's voices contributing to this particular conversation. Given the life-and-death issues black families have to face, it feels petty to publicly express my annoyance over what sometimes happens at home. Also, Birdsong's words are in my mind: domestic duties are more often shared by black men. Cat Brooks, a longtime political organizer in Oakland who is also a mother and wife, has another take on this.

"This is where I get in trouble with traditional feminists," she tells me. "A piece of my fighting for liberation is taking care of my black man." Brooks's husband is from Trinidad, and his formal education only went through the eighth grade, she tells me. He's a master carpenter and electrician, but he "struggles to stay consistently employed because he's black and immigrant." When I mention invisible labor to Brooks, she rejects the frame outright. "He gets his ass kicked every time he walks out the door. Not that we [black women] don't, but it's just different. If he can come home and the bed is made and I've done the laundry and I put the shit away, and he can walk into a clean house where he can just sit down on the couch and exhale, I'm good with that."

Brooks echoes something Angela Davis researched and wrote decades ago about enslaved women's domestic work in the slave quarters: that it was powerful because it was solely about the survival and comfort of black people. "In the infinite anguish of ministering to the needs of the men and children around her . . . she was performing the only labor of the slave community which could not be directly and immediately claimed by the oppressor . . . Domestic labor was the only meaningful labor for the slave community as a whole."[26]

Whether we strive to create a domestic refuge for partners who face daily disrespect or work long hours while our children's dad stays home with the kids, the realities of black family life are obscured. What we've had instead of self-generated reports from inside actual black families are news and opinion that consistently misrepresent black life. This misrepresentation is damaging. We need to see reflections of ourselves as we truly are to feel confident that we're not alone, that we're not the exception to the rule, and that we as black people actually have lessons to offer others in how to form resilient, functional families. I want Is to have access to media and pop culture that reflect that CDC data on black fathers' involvement in their kids' lives, because that data is in line with her own experience. Instead, and unsurprisingly, a recent study of how families are represented in local and national media found that in news images, black fathers were shown spending time with their kids almost half as often as white fathers.[27] The study was conducted by the University of Illinois at Urbana-Champaign communications professor Travis L. Dixon and commissioned by the social justice organizations Color of Change and Family Story. Released in late 2017, the study reviewed outlets including Fox News, CNN, the *New York Times*, and the *Atlanta Journal Constitution* and found that media generally paint white families as sources of social stability—educated, upwardly mobile, entrepreneurial. These same news and opinion media portray black families as sources of social instability—criminal, impoverished, and lacking respect for accepted social values. For example, the study found that black families make up less than a third of poor families in the United States but represent around 60 percent in news and opinion media. White families make up two-thirds of the poor, but our media tells us these folks don't exist.

Luckily, we're in an era when Issa Rae, Shonda Rhimes, Ava DuVernay, Terence Nance, Mara Brock Akil, Kenya Barris, and other black storytellers have huge pop cultural platforms and can create new, nuanced narratives. News and opinion too often fail when it comes to reflecting the intimate contours of black life. That the majority of households headed by unmarried women actually live above the poverty line, regardless of race or ethnicity, is one example.[28] But if you only followed news media, you'd think we don't exist, especially if we're black. Once the stories of our thriving, or at least of living with many of the same challenges that married couples with kids have, are told, then the focus can be on poverty itself rather than on single motherhood.

But the complex story of family formation and black mothering isn't only about beating back stigma and correcting falsehoods. The psychic and emotional impact of leading households on our own is often ignored, and I've been guilty of this myself. In writing about black women and marriage in the past, I've failed to acknowledge that some of us actually aspire to the narratives of being chosen, of living happily ever after. Yes, it's important that we can and do successfully raise children without steady, committed romantic partners. But can we also note how depressing it is that we so often have to? There's a reason some black women were excited when finally, after twelve seasons of the franchise, there was a black Bachelorette. Some of us want love, marriage, and a baby carriage in exactly that order and preferably with black men. It's important to acknowledge how it feels when those desires are often out of reach for us in a way they're just not for other women.

Add to the existential angst the day-to-day responsibility of being in charge, which can overwhelm. Even with family help and enough money to pay for childcare, it's exhausting to be the sole adult responsible for cooking, bathing, reading, playing, and cleaning on those days or in those stretches of hours when you're going it alone. I never take it for granted that I was 100 percent certain I wanted to be a mother when I had my daughter. I can't imagine giving mothering the energy it demands and deserves if I had come into this reluctantly, especially now that it's often just the two of us. I enjoy the work of mothering and don't often feel like I'm going through the motions or putting on a brave face, but there have been times when my spirit has flagged under the weight. I'm reminded of those times, the moments I've blinked back tears when I read asha bandele's memoir *Something Like Beautiful*, which is about raising her daughter while her husband is incarcerated and then deported. She writes:

> I told myself if I cried I was setting a bad example for my daughter. Others told me the very same thing. Told me never to be a victim, Black women are not victims and we are not weak. Tossed aside is Michele Wallace's brilliant feminist tome about why Black women have always been, but should never have been, asked to be superwomen. In the post-welfare-reform days of the alpha mom, I was clear that being a victim, showing any weakness, was punishable by complete isolation and total loss of respect. I was a mother, a single mother, a single Black mother. I was part of a tradition of women who do not bend and who do not break. This is what I said, this is how I now defined myself. As someone with no room for error.[29]

I see little room for error in my own life. I have to guard against letting parenting become one more place I practice perfectionism. There are so many reasons to try to do it as close to perfectly as possible, since the mainstream conversation tells me that as both an unmarried mom and the child of an unmarried mom, I'm incapable of being or raising a successful, well-adjusted person. Even though I have known since childhood how mean-spirited and hollow that conversation is, I'm still affected by the stigma. As I get older, I can also see the danger in being too defensive, in disproving others' assumptions before I honestly explore my own nuanced truths. Where do I find space to be vulnerable and acknowledge the hurt without giving into the narrative that I am of and in a "broken family" and thus a broken person destined to raise a broken child?

It's a February day, and Is and I are at the playground. I push her on the swing and notice that she can't take her eyes off the next swing over, where a dad is pushing his daughter. I think to myself: I know that feeling. That "Why don't I have that?" feeling. That "Where's *my* dad?" feeling. That "I want bigger, messier, gruffer, rougher and sillier than Mom" feeling. The truth is I'm projecting. My child is a watcher; she's super nosy and could be thinking anything. She actually gets playground time with her dad, though not daily. But my mind goes there because I am still, at thirty-nine, processing my own feelings around abandonment and loss. I don't want that for my daughter. I don't want her to know that sense of longing. If she does, I want her to know she can express it, put it out in the open. In my experience, the silence around an absence can do more harm than the absence itself.

In 2007, artist Meshell Ndegeocello released an album called *The World Has Made Me the Man of My Dreams*. I think about that album's title a lot. There is something about learning to navigate an often-inhospitable world on one's own and with the help of relatives and friends that can make us into our own rock-solid protectors. Partnership with a man can begin to feel unnecessary, nice when it comes along but not a must for survival or happiness. This strength can be a source of pride, but it can also be reason to grieve when one starts to think about all the structural and historical reasons black women have had to be so independent and black men have often been unavailable or unwilling to offer meaningful help.

Aya de Leon has taken all this heavy history, all these stats, all this theory, and her own heart's desires into account as she's formed her family. The Berkeley, California–based writer and academic was born into a multiracial family of artists: her mother is Puerto Rican, blonde, and often mistaken for white. Her father is African American. De Leon knew that she wanted a black family comprised of a black partner and a black child. Nurturing and maintaining a loving, black family is part of her life's work. "I think it's part of this larger activist project, like can black people love each other and stay together? Can black people be committed to each other?" she says. "It's not a better project than the project of being a single mom and making your life go well or being a mom who's married to or in relationship with someone who's not black. It's just—that's my project."

In 1997, when she was in her late twenties, de Leon wrote an essay in *Essence* about being without a romantic partner and getting married anyway. She married herself in a small wedding ceremony to publicly celebrate her commitment to and love for herself.[30] Twenty years later, married and with a child, she sees the gaps between what she as a younger feminist expected from relationships and what she has come to expect now. "There's a particular piece around dealing with the kind of trauma that black men carry," she tells me. She recalls being young and "not really understanding the kinds of struggles that men have in their lives around being present, being connected, negotiating, sharing power."

Now she allies with her nine-year-old daughter to identify the ways sexism shows up in their home. This includes looking critically with her daughter at who does what work around the house. "I'm committed to her resisting my domination, and I'm really committed to her resisting her father's domination," de Leon says.

I have always been baffled by marriage. Even after two decades of committed adult relationships, I marvel at others' ability to legally bind themselves to someone who's supposed to simultaneously fill roles that typically have nothing to do with each other—sex partner, financial partner, partner in nightly dinner conversation. But listening to de Leon describe family as a way of reclaiming black intimacy despite the oppressive forces that have worked to destroy it, I see the allure.

"It's not always like, 'Am I having fun? Am I living my best life in this moment?'" she says, laughing. "Sometimes it means hanging through periods where I might not hang in there if I hadn't made that commitment."

CHAPTER 4

Play

AROUND IS'S FIRST BIRTHDAY AND INCREASINGLY AS SHE NEARS EIGHT-
een months, I start thinking a lot about the need to get her
around other children. She is the first and only child to her
father and to me, and we don't have her in daycare. Instead,
since birth she has divided her days between one-on-one
time with me, her dad, her grandmothers, and college-aged
babysitters who come to our home.

I'm an only child and bristle at age-old accusations that
only children are selfish, maladjusted misanthropes destined
to lonely lives.[1] But I also know that the conditions of my
childhood provided me with a socially rich experience that
not a lot of singletons can claim. Because my maternal grandparents had eight children, I had a lot of first cousins right
around my age, all of whom lived in the same city as me during most of our childhoods. Weekend sleepovers at the home
of one aunt or another were a common occurrence, and we
were often together on holidays—not just Christmas and
Thanksgiving but Memorial and Labor Days, birthdays, and

the occasional Saturday or Sunday afternoon. I had peers to team up with, who would teach and tease me as the occasion demanded.

My neighborhood was filled with an even larger collection of cousins with whom I could play and explore our immediate surroundings. We'd ride our bikes the mile or so to the Civil War–era canon with the plaque that told the story of the Union troops who had trained on the land before crossing the Ohio River to fight in the South. We'd walk to the make-shift petting zoo where goats roamed behind the Schoolhouse Restaurant, an actual former schoolhouse that my grandfather had attended. We'd go fishing in the Little Miami River and practice our penny drops and other gymnastic feats on the metal railings in front of the church down the street. These cousins were blood relations. My great-great-grandparents had settled in the neighborhood along with an array of their own siblings and cousins, and I grew up playing with the grandchildren of my grandfather's first cousins and an assortment of other neighborhood kids. During the summers, we would leave home soon after breakfast to meet up and then bike or walk the quiet streets until lunchtime. We'd meet up after that meal and do it all over again until dusk fell, when we knew dinner was waiting at home.

But everything is different now. Few of us live in Camp Dennison, and some of my cousins have moved out of town. I had a child on the late side at thirty-eight, and my peers' children tend to be older than Is. Is's father has one sister, and she doesn't have children. So my daughter is growing up with-out the benefit of a child-rich, tight-knit community or a big extended family filled with kids her age. In the absence of the readymade peer group that I had, I know I'll need to create one. Like most parents, I'm driven in part by a need for childcare. But even more, I'm driven by a desire to enrich her life, to give her opportunities to be creative and to play.

With those early opportunities for play, creativity, and learning come a child's initial socialization. I'm conscious of this as Is begins to interact with her world. "Socialization"— the very word feels fraught with unacknowledged meaning. I look it up and find that its use traces back to the mid-eighteenth century, and it means "to make suitable for society." What does it mean to become suitable for a society that isn't really suitable for you? If I am often confronted with evidence that our society doesn't respect black children as children or black adults as humans, what does it mean to prepare someone for this place? Why help my black daughter internalize our society's values and norms when so many of our dominant ideologies are antiblack and antiwoman? Yes, she has to survive here, and it's my job to teach her how to do that. But there is a fine line between surviving the world and accepting it as it is. I don't want her to assimilate to the point that she loses the ability to see and challenge what is wrong around her.

Psychiatrist Alvin Poussaint consulted on *The Cosby Show* and collaborated with Bill Cosby on his 2007 bible of black respectability politics, *Come On, People*. In addition to providing some of the intellectual underpinnings to Cosby's racial uplift project, Poussaint was known as a kind of Dr. Spock within black communities in the 1980s and 1990s. I read his

1992 book, *Raising Black Children*, coauthored with psychiatrist James Comer, and see that I'm not the first person to grapple with this question: "Many black parents question and have mixed feelings about passing on the values and ways of a society that says in so many ways, 'We do not value black men and women, boys and girls, as much as we do whites . . .' The need to preserve our culture and community springs from a desire to maintain a real and psychological place, where we are accepted, respected and protected. For this reason we are concerned about whether 'white psychology and child-rearing approaches' will change us, hurt us, destroy our culture."[2]

When my daughter is an infant, I prioritize maintaining "a real and psychological place, where [she is] accepted, respected and protected." I work freelance and take an unpaid maternity leave for the first three months of her life. I put my contracts on hold and don't accept any new assignments. For the six months after that, her father and I take turns working and caring for her. He works afternoons and evenings; I work in the early part of each weekday. Until she's nine months old she's solely in the care of her dad, her grandmothers, and myself. It's during this time that I apply what I've read in child-development books and also lean in to learning how to parent from my mom, Is's paternal grandmother, and the other elder women in our lives. Her paternal grandmother encourages us to let Is do things on her own. She nudges us to make her feed herself with a spoon and eventually clean up her toys and walk up and down steps on her own. Sometimes I think she's introducing some skill or task too soon, and I can't see what the rush is. But as Is gets old enough to better grasp whatever skill or concept, I see how her growing independence makes my life a little easier. I have fewer heavy things to carry if she walks more. I can eat or clean up the kitchen if Is can feed herself.

My mom teaches me how to parent in part by just putting the necessary tools around me before I even know that I need them. Around Is's first birthday, she brings over training underwear and a potty. She doesn't tell me I should start potty training or make me feel like I'm falling behind in my parenting duties. Both grandmothers just start doing things themselves and make sure I see the progress Is makes. When my aunt Yvonne watches her for a month after childcare unexpectedly falls through, I see how the drop-off goes much easier if Is is immediately led into an activity she likes, in that case, helping my aunt water her plants. With further proof that distraction and redirection can help cut down the number of meltdowns, I start using it in other contexts.

In her book *The Importance of Being Little: What Preschoolers Really Need from Grownups*, early-childhood educator Erika Christakis emphasizes the role family plays in a child's early learning. She quotes at length from a 1974 parenting book to illustrate that despite our current focus on formal enrichment experiences in the years before kindergarten, kids used to learn "innumerable skills and acquired an encyclopedic amount of information . . . words, number concepts, rhyme, plain facts" just from spending time with family members.[3]

For as long as I can remember, Is and I have taken long walks together, meandering around our neighborhood just north of downtown Cincinnati. When she is around eight months old, I start pointing out the things I like to look at, attempting to draw her attention there as well. We stroll past a rose bush in bloom and I situate her stroller so that she can reach out and touch the petals. "Look at the flowers, honey" becomes "Look at the red flowers, honey" and then "How many red flowers, honey?" as she moves from infant to toddler. I use the walks to show her how things change, how the sunflower high up on a stalk in a neighbor's yard could be so radiant and strong one day and, just weeks later, bow its head and drop its leaves under the weight of age.

When she is around a year and a half, she starts to express her preferences on the route, first pointing in a particular direction, grunting, and whining for a bit if I choose a different path. Then, at twenty months: "That way, Mama!" The walks and our stops at various playgrounds become one of the many ways I track her development. Around the same time these first halting sentences appear, so does her ability to climb the steps of a play structure, sit down at the top of the slide, and come down on her own. Just a few weeks before, I hovered behind her every step of the way, nervous that she might plummet to the ground.

And, of course, we're always reading. It's fascinating to watch what from a book burrows into her memory. In a whimsical, bilingual Yuyi Morales book about Frida Kahlo, Frida bandages the wounded, bleeding leg of a deer. I explain that the deer is hurt, and so "hurt" becomes the word she uses for any deer she sees and a favorite word in general. I don't pull her pants up quickly enough for her tastes after a diaper change? "Hurt!" The straps on her car seat are uncomfortable?

"That hurt!" She delights over the familiarity of the sun ("hot," never "sun"), birds, anything that goes "roar!" No sooner can I say "the end" than I hear "Again! More!" a two-punch command that shows up right around twenty months as well.

Singing and dancing have also been part of our repertoire. When she was a newborn, I'd put on Cesaria Evora and rock Is in the nursing chair, hopeful that the Cape Verdean crooning was priming her ear for Portuguese and other languages. When she was still in her pumpkin seat, I'd put her on the kitchen table and make up dance routines while I cooked. I'd put on Héctor Lavoe or Beyoncé and hold her while we danced around the kitchen. Now that she can play more independently, she'll hear a song and stop what she's doing to move to the beat. She recently asked my mom to play a Drake song she loves. "That's my jam," Is told her.

Is brings so much joy and humor into our lives, and I hope she feels the same about us. In watching her learn the world around her, I learn her personality and I see the world anew. In our daily tangle of movement, noise, spontaneity, and silliness, I see her balancing independence with attachment. I see her venturing out to satisfy her curiosity while keeping close the people and things that give her comfort. I remember that Maria Montessori, the Italian educator, advised adults to "follow the child," and I observe Is as a way to learn more about who and how she is, what she's drawn to. Of course, sometimes I have to lead her in directions she doesn't want to go.

When she's around eighteen months old, we start watching around fifteen minutes of *Sesame Street* every day. Up to that point, I'd been adamant that Is shouldn't be in front of any screen at any time for any reason. Education reporter Anya Kamenetz's book, *The Art of Screen Time: How Your Family Can Balance Digital Media and Real Life*, on children and screen time had recently come out, and I listened to her discuss her findings on NPR and a tech podcast called *Note to Self*. While so much about the effect of digital media on children seemed open to debate, one thing seemed clear: kids Is's age shouldn't use screens unless they're for video chatting. But as the mother of a black girl whose tightly curled hair was getting thicker and longer, I needed to figure out how to keep her from scrambling away, batting at my hands, and screaming long enough to get her hair done. In search of advice, I posted a hand-wringing plea to a Facebook group made up mostly of moms of color and moms from immigrant families. I acknowledged all my fears: that I was prioritizing a socially enforced expectation that my daughter's hair look neat over her developmentally appropriate fidgeting. That embarking on a journey of caring for my black daughter's hair was bringing up all my childhood angst around styles and discomfort and texture and length. I got around eighty responses from the Facebook group of nearly seven thousand people. The most common advice was this: Doing hair is simply part of keeping black children looking cared for. Relax and give your child a screen to distract her while you braid her head.

This is how I came to discover that you can watch catchy *Sesame Street* song after catchy *Sesame Street* song on YouTube. First we discovered Feist counting to four in the most melodic way. From there, Destiny's Child drove home the meaning of the verb "walk," we listened to Michelle Obama tell Grover about the benefits of a healthy breakfast, and Halle Berry, along with Elmo and a tiger, broke down the word "nibble." As I write this, I'm humming a song we listened to during this morning's hair session, "Raise Your Hand Up High," which features a puppet explaining the appropriate way to respond to a teacher in the classroom.

The hair situation helped me check my own habit of being rigidly attached to expert advice and confirmed one truth of parenting: you're not going to do it "right" all the time. Sometimes you cave to what's easiest and most convenient for you as the parent, and that's how you stay sane.

When Is is nine months old and her dad's work schedule changes, we hire help. Like all parents, I'm nervous about leaving my child in the care of a stranger. Race adds an additional layer to my trepidation. Christakis, the author and early-childhood educator, writes that "high quality relationships are the best indicator of quality child care" and that "we shouldn't underestimate the pedagogic power of deeply loving care."[4] In her list of what parents should look for in evaluating a daycare center, she places at the top, "close, affectionate interactions between caregivers and children, including frequent laughter and hugs." I have read the reports that black children are more than twice as likely as other children to be suspended or expelled from preschool.[5] We're not in preschool yet, but it makes sense to me that the same bias and blind spots that compel white early-childhood educators to unnecessarily kick a three- or four-year-old out of school would be present in white nannies and babysitters as well.

I hire only black caregivers or those who I perceive to be on the margins in some way that will predispose them to see our humanity. Each time I need help, I post some version of this listing to Care.com, the online matchmaker for families and caregivers:

> Cincinnati family seeks a nanny available Wed., Thurs., and Fri. 10–5. You will care for a twenty-month-old toddler in a Northside home. Our child is curious, observant, active, and engaged. She loves being read to and taking walks in the neighborhood when weather allows. We are seeking a nurturing caregiver who has experience in racially diverse and multicultural environments and experience leading child development activities with toddlers. We are a low TV/ screen family and emphasize healthy eating and outdoor activity. Some food preparation and light housekeeping (washing dishes related to the child's meals, keeping play areas tidy) required.

No one ever responds with a mention of their experience in "racially diverse and multicultural environments," so I screen applicants to see who both fits our needs and is phenotypically of color or has a name that implies that they're from a recently arrived immigrant family. If someone mentions having worked at a childcare facility that I know to serve a lot of black families, I'm interested regardless of their race. Otherwise, I discriminate on the basis of what I can discern about applicants' race, ethnicity, and culture. This person will be in our home alone with a child who can't later tell me if something has gone wrong. I worry that my child will be given an offensive nickname or that her hair will be touched with a kind of disgusted curiosity. I worry that diapers changes will be delayed or meals skipped because this person can't see my child as fully human or vulnerable.

It's about my comfort as well. Some days, this person will come into our home when I'm still in pajamas, my house upside down. I feel uncomfortable displaying the imperfections of my domestic life to white people who aren't longtime friends. One day, I am prepping lunch and trying to get out the door, and Is is upset. One of our babysitters is there, soothing Is in her lap and quietly singing along while Lalah Hathaway belts "Angel." It's a moment that demonstrates a cultural congruence, and it feels good.

Our search for care often takes a little longer because of my preferences. I turn to my mom, who worked full-time throughout my childhood and didn't have flexibility in hours or the ability to work from home. When I was a baby, I alternately stayed with my grandmother, my great-grandmother, and elder black women who were family friends. Then my mom enrolled me in a preschool at a church that was a ten-minute drive from our home. I remember that we memorized the books of the Bible there. I ask what memories she has of the place.

She says she chose it because it was close to home, so convenient for drop-offs and pick-ups, and because the teacher-to-student ratio seemed good. I ask if she was concerned, either then or during my subsequent K–12 education, that I didn't have any black teachers. No, she tells me.

She hadn't either throughout her own education, so it hadn't been a concern. And she hadn't been gripped by worries that I'd be mistreated, as I am now regarding Is. Instead, my mother counted on her own vigilance and involvement to send a signal to teachers and administrators that our family was not to be messed with. Because of her work hours, she couldn't do things like join the PTA or volunteer in the classroom. But she stayed in phone communication with my teachers between evening open houses and parent-teacher conferences and felt that being an involved and watchful parent could act as a deterrent to racially motivated mistreatment.

I take from this advice that I should relax a little and trust myself more, but I'd like to feel more excited about my daughter's first exposure to an educational environment. I'd rather have a "this will be great" attitude than "they better not try it" apprehensions lurking in the back of my mind. When I think of where black parents can approach their children's early education with this kind of optimism, I think of Little Maroons. In my research, the Brooklyn-based preschool and after-school program comes up again and again. Maroon communities in the African diaspora were established by formerly enslaved people who escaped and set up independent settlements. Maroons had to stay ready to defend themselves against the looming threat of reenslavement. The childcare cooperative's name says a lot about what families it's for, politically and culturally. According to its website, the co-op operates "from a child-led, African-centered curriculum rooted in indigenous wisdom." My friend rashid shabazz and his wife, Rashida, send their daughter there. The girl has attended as a complement to other preschool and primary school programs, shabazz tells me, and it's given her a community where she can learn about freedom fighters and feel affirmed. "Little Maroons has provided that space of being loved up on, which is really the key," shabazz says.

Adjoa Jones de Almeida is one of the co-op's founders. Her children are now sixteen and twelve; more than a decade ago, Jones de Almeida and her husband joined with five other families who were active in social justice and black liberation organizing to lay the groundwork for the collective. She remembers the group reflecting on critical questions in those early days: What would the curriculum look like? Would there be paid staff? How much cultural content should the program include? The founders brought different ideas about how much to emphasize academic rigor versus creativity and social development. "I remember . . . some folks [saying], 'We need to start them reading,'" Jones de Almeida says. Her own mother had helped start a school without walls in a Brazilian mountain town and had later enrolled Jones de Almeida in a progressive Waldorf school, an approach to education that encourages unstructured, creative play in the early years. "Me with my hippie-dippie mom, I was like, 'No, no, no we can't rush them. Let them play.'"

Monifa Bandele, a mother and organizer in Brooklyn whose daughters are now sixteen and nineteen, is also a cofounder, along with her husband, and remembers those early conversations. She credits Jones de Almeida's Waldorf background with helping the other founding families understand that toddlers need to explore their environments and practice gross motor skills and that the reading, sitting still, and perfecting fine motor skills can come later.

During her own childhood, Bandele's father, who had been a member of the Black Panther Party, worked to build independent African-centered schools. She and her husband were educated in these schools, often called *shules*. When it came to creating Little Maroons, the founding families knew that the co-op would be African centered, but they also knew they wanted to leave behind some of what had been common-place in the shules of the 1970s and 1980s, such as the use of corporal punishment and a patriarchal and heteronormative culture. Bandele remembers standing with other girl students with hands crossed and heads bowed while the boys stood at attention. "It was a hypermasculine environment," she remembers, and early conversations around Little Maroons addressed how to leave behind the chauvinism while teaching their children to value black institutions. Years ago, the cooperative started with a group of two- to five-year-olds gathering at the Bandeles' home to be taught by their parents on a rotating schedule. Even now that her children are in high school and college, she looks back at Little Maroons as being a place that reinforced her family's political and cultural values.

As far as I can tell, there's nothing like a Little Maroons in Cincinnati, and I'm not ready to try to organize a preschool co-op. Still, I know it's time to get Is around other children more regularly so that she can have more fun. I also want to make sure she's hitting the developmental milestones that she's supposed to, and I need to be around other adults with kids or early childcare experts to better know what those are. Just

after Is turns one, I start taking her to two weekly groups—
one a story and song circle at a branch of the public library, the
other a weekly, forty-five-minute class called Music Together.
I figure this is where we'll begin the process of socialization.

On Wednesdays at 10:00 a.m., the children's librarian at
a nearby branch takes his guitar and a basket full of board
books into a bright solarium. Moms, along with some grandparents and nannies, gather there with babies and toddlers in
tow to listen to a few stories and sing along while the librarian strums his guitar and leads classics like "Twinkle, Twinkle
Little Star." Every circle ends with a rousing rendition of "Old
McDonald" in which every caregiver or child takes turns
shouting out a preferred farm animal, prompting the rest of
us to make the accompanying sound. (At home when we sing
it, I change the words to "and on her farm she had a," another
small effort to keep Is's mind open to the possibility that jobs
aren't gendered.)

We like library story time. Is is starting to know the various animal sounds, and her face lights up with recognition
as we all "neigh" and "baa" and "moo" in unison. The librarian
greets us by name and with a smile when we walk in, and Is
and I often stick around after the forty-five-minute session is
over to play with the toys in the room and be around the other
straggler parents and kids. I want Is to feel that the library is
hers. I want her to understand early that she has access to as
much knowledge and entertainment as she can handle, and
she doesn't even have to pay for it. I still remember going to
Cincinnati's libraries with my mom as a child, and I want
those memories for Is as well.

That same autumn after she turns one, we start a class called Music Together. It's an early-childhood music and movement curriculum that's available in three thousand locations around the world, according to its website. Local teachers train in how to lead small groups and then run their own franchises. I've talked to friends in other cities, from Detroit to San Francisco, who've gone to a Music Together class with a child in their lives. Our class is led by a Malaysian-born music teacher who is warm, patient, and energetic. She leads the group with an acoustic guitar in her lap while a dozen or so pairs of adults and kids circle up with her, seated cross-legged on the floor.

Each class opens with "Hello Song" and closes with "Goodbye, So Long, Farewell," both of which invite the class to say a hello or goodbye to each child by name. They're rituals meant to make each child feel welcome and to teach the basics of polite interaction—that it's good to say, "So glad to see you" as a greeting and that a hug or handshake is an appropriate way to part with a friend. Between these two bookends, we sing and move around to other songs, some accompanied by our teacher, others set to recorded instrumentation. At the first class, each family receives a CD with two dozen songs that will be sung over the course of the session. Some are familiar—songs like "This Old Man," "Hey, Diddle, Diddle," and "Greensleeves."

One morning I'm singing a song from class and trying to engage Is while video chatting with her dad. Recognizing the lyrics, he pulls up a recording of Nina Simone singing "Li'l Liza Jane." It's a song I'd never heard before it came remixed in a Music Together offering punctuated with African drums and called "Funga Alafia." I play the class CD in the car to get Is used to the music, and eventually it becomes a way to soothe her. I hear her singing along or at least making sounds that approximate what she's hearing. I come to have my own favorites and cheer a little inside whenever a song on the CD features Grandma Yvette, an older black woman whose voice transports me to the church choirs I heard as a kid.

I think about this a lot as Is and I begin to touch into the wider world. So many of today's social and political problems are rooted in the ways that whiteness, maleness, heterosexuality, and being cisgender have historically been centered in our culture and considered normal. Now that I have a child, I see more clearly all the ways we're taught what perspectives and voices to listen to and trust early in our lives. This is one reason why Is's bookshelves are filled with books that feature black and brown and bilingual characters and girls and women as protagonists. In our Music Together class, we sing a song called "Every Day." Its lyrics annoy me: "Mommies wake up / Daddies wake up / Babies wake up / I wake up . . . Girls get busy / Boys get busy / Babies get busy / I get busy." Mommies, daddies, and babies stretch, get hungry, get tired, all as a way of teaching the normal rhythms of a day. It's innocuous on its face, but these earliest teachings about how to classify people make it hard for older children and adults to comprehend a person who's gender nonconforming or who uses pronouns other than "she" and "he." It's a cognitive leap I struggle to make myself, and my own socialization is to blame. And as for the song's repetition of who's home every day, what about kids whose mommies or daddies work third shift or are locked up or just absent?

The class has its shortcomings, but it's also a godsend in part because it gives me something I need as an exhausted, often overwhelmed new parent: forty-five minutes when I can turn my mind off for a while. Someone else is in charge, picking the songs, leading the dances, engaging the kids. Both here and at library story time, I look around the circles and see other parents and caregivers with vacant looks on their faces, glad for the respite offered by another grown-up paying attention to their child, so they can fall back a little. The music class is also helpful because there I pick up a few more parenting skills. One day when class has finished, the teacher sees me struggling to get Is into her coat, hat, and mittens. My daughter wants to run around the room instead. The teacher comes over and starts singing a version of one of the songs we sing in class: "She'll be puttin' on her coat when she comes / She'll be puttin' one arm in when she comes / Then she'll put the other hand in when she comes." Is is mesmerized by the description of what she's doing set to a melody she recognizes, and I've learned a way to cut five minutes off the often-arduous routine of getting my child ready to go outside in the cold.

❧

IN CHRISTAKIS'S BOOK ON PRESCHOOL, I COME ACROSS A relevant quote from theorist Len Vygotsky: "Play is 'not an activity but a source of development.'"[6] Her book is focused on children ages three to five, but reading it when Is is around eighteen months helps me know what to watch for in her upcoming development, including so-called preacademic skills like whether she can follow directions or share materials when seated at a table with classmates. "Even observing a child decide where to play can reveal volumes about her ability to plan, self-regulate and communicate," Christakis writes.

I get a chance to observe Is at play with other children when I enroll her in a toddler enrichment program at a nearby private school. On an April morning dusted with snow, I rush our morning routine to get us there on time. It's taken me weeks to learn how to do this: She'll go to her grandmother's for four hours after the class is finished—work time for me—so pack lunch the night before. Also braid her hair the night before. Whisk her directly from bed to high chair for oatmeal. Curriculum aside, the class is helpful just to get me in the swing of getting Is to school with ease.

After we're buzzed into the building, she stares up at the older students' colorful work papering the hallway walls. I open the child gate, and we walk into the space that's home to the school's toddler and two-year-old preschool program. One of the two teachers is standing near the door to greet us. She asks how Is is, holds out her hand, and Is touches it. I am struck by how preternaturally happy she and the other teacher are. I've never seen either one without a smile, same with the librarian and the music teacher. Radiating joy and patience should be a requirement for working with young kids. It certainly helps put me at ease, as I'm sure it does Is. I take her coat and hat off and then stash them in a cubby with her name on it, along with her diaper bag and my bulky winter coat.

The rooms are set up with little stations for the kids to explore: Play-Doh and different tools to shape it, toddler-sized couches, a reading nook, a little table with a wide, shallow box full of lima beans that the kids can scoop up or run their fingers through—opportunities for "sensory play," one of the teachers explains to me. There are big bins of toys everywhere and a small wooden play structure. The kids can climb the stairs, crouch down to crawl through a short tube, and then slide to the floor.

Is walks to one of the tables set up with a sensory activity. Some clear, gel-like substance lies on a wet-looking tray. There are tiny plastic tools that look like scalpels and pizza cutter wheels arranged on the tray as well. A teacher crouches down to the level at which Is is seated on a tiny chair. "You can cut like this . . . Maybe it's easier to use this side," she says and flips the tool to see which results in the quicker cut. I watch to see whether and how Is picks up the tools. Using them seems to require more pressure than she can apply, and she handles the gel pieces instead, feeling their texture and turning them over to examine them from various angles.

Because we've been coming to this class long enough, and because I've observed other toddler programs, I understand that the point of such activities is to get the kids to work on using their hands in specific ways. That way, the theory goes, they'll be ready when it's time to learn to write with a pencil, cut with scissors, or do other tasks that require a strong pincer grasp and other controlled movements. One table over, there's a big goopy blob-like substance with little glittery balls mixed throughout. At another table, the kids can use watercolor paints on coffee filters to create little earths covered in pastel swirls of oceans and continents. It would never occur to me to set up crafting activities around the house, and it's here I learn that if I put Is in her high chair with a bowl filled with popcorn kernels or rice and a measuring spoon, I can keep her occupied while I make dinner. I also learn it's easier for a toddler to draw on paper that's set up on an easel or affixed to the wall than on paper placed flat on the floor or a table.

During the class, parents and nannies are seated or crouched next to their kids or else supervise from afar, depending on the kids' age and temperament. One boy who I'd guess to be around two and a half is clearly mom dependent. I first notice when he's dropped one of the cutting tools on the floor, just out of reach. "Do you need help?" I ask. Then, noticing how close his hand is, I say, "Looks like you've almost got it." When I see that he's still struggling to get it, I pick it up for him, and he puts it right back down on the ground and then swivels around to continue trying to get his mom's attention. I see that he's hoarded all the gel pieces in front of himself, and when Is takes one to play with, he's turned toward his mom again, frowning and gesturing frantically that something has gone awry.

Besides the skills acquisition, this is the big reason we're here: How do other kids act? How does Is respond to what they do? What is actually the right amount to intervene? What can I tell about her temperament? Does she lose it when challenged? Does she melt down in tears or get aggressive? Does she scratch or bite, which is what she does to me when she's overly tired and frustrated?

And how do the other parents act? We are the only black family in the class. There are a couple of families that I perceive as nonwhite, though I don't know how they identify. Mostly these are Spanish-speaking moms and grandmas with their toddlers. There is a South Asian mom of twins from Chicago who I chat with a lot. The cars that I see pull out after class ends are mostly Lexus SUVs, BMWs. Across lines of race, ethnicity, and class, we are united in our exhaustion and by the frantic way we are trying hard not to let our kid be *that* kid. In between trying to teach our children how to eat with a fork, how to use a toilet, how to walk without falling too much, we come to this place once a week to also try to teach our kids how to be civil and friendly, even when they don't feel like it.

I think this is even more complex for parents of black children. While I love how spirited and direct Is can be, I don't want her to be saddled with the behavioral labels so often put on black girls. I remember getting feedback from adults at my predominately white school about how I showed up in the world. My teachers—mostly white women—often told me to smile, which confused me. I wasn't unhappy, but I also wasn't particularly bubbly. In retrospect, I was thoughtful and a tad melancholy at times. But the message I received was that my face's default setting made others uncomfortable and that I should put on a false face to put others at ease. Black girls with so-called attitudes are assumed to be angry black women in the making, and so our socialization sometimes includes having the expressions on our faces policed and learning very early how to get them under control.

It's also in our toddler enrichment class that I catch myself modeling a survival technique that Is hasn't shown that she needs yet. I'm not much for rules that, if disregarded, put neither myself nor other people in harm's way. I like finding shortcuts and workarounds to make my life smoother. If everyone's told to zig, I zag, knowing the lines will be shorter and there will be fewer people for whom I'll need to force a perfunctory smile. It's not surprising, then, that I find myself hearing directions at the enrichment program but unconsciously choosing to tweak them for our purposes. Example: The lead teacher asks for help getting out the carpet squares onto which the toddlers are to put their bottoms and starts singing the circle time song:

> *Everybody have a seat, have a seat, have a seat*
> *Everybody have a seat on the floor*
> *Not on the ceiling, not on the door*
> *Everybody have a seat on the floor*

But in my mind, I hear: "It's going to take a minute to corral all these kids. Perfect bathroom break time." Or "Ugh, I saw Is touch something that little boy sneezed on earlier. Time to wash hands." There's nothing inherently wrong about this move. Body breaks need to get in where they can. But Is is a sponge, and if every time some group directive is issued, I ignore it, she's going to pick up on and internalize that. I don't typically think of myself as included in "Hey, you, everybody," and maybe this aligns with my skeptical attitude toward authority. I want her to have that same sense of autonomy and ability to know whether or not her needs match the group's. But I think you have to learn the rules before you can effectively break them. So I decide to do my best to follow instructions here, for Is's sake.

This gets to the heart of my complex feelings around the word "socialization." Like "civilization," it feels cryptically racist, used to further the aims of people who want to maintain their own ideas of who's more advanced, more human, more worthy. Yes, of course, I want my daughter to know how to greet people and say goodbye. I want her to use polite words like "please" and "thank you." I want her to recognize the feeling of being welcome so that she can make others feel welcome and understand the value of hospitality and kindness. I don't want her to scratch or bite or hit her classmates. I don't have a problem with most of the values and norms that are being transmitted to Is now, but I know this will change at some point. She'll be taught to stand and recite the Pledge of Allegiance. She'll be subjected to school dress codes that impose retrograde standards of femininity and propriety. As the mother of a black girl, I want her to be able to quickly recognize when she is being mistreated or manipulated so that she can act accordingly and protect herself. This means being able to identify when being polite or bowing to authority isn't the right thing to do.

CHAPTER 5

Belonging

I NEVER WANT IS TO FEEL THAT IT'S HER AGAINST THE WORLD. I NEVER want her to be so skeptical of the status quo that she's isolated, boxed out of social groups by those who consider her to be an overly critical killjoy. I remember a black boy with whom I went to middle school who wasn't from the tight-knit neighborhood in which I grew up. He never stood up during the Pledge of Allegiance. He was solemn, kept to himself, and observed from a remove the spectacle of our suburban school, which was like something out of a John Hughes movie. He made fun of me for teaching my white friends the Electric Slide. He haughtily steeled himself against the possibility of mistreatment or misunderstanding, and I imagine those days were lonely for him. My own undeveloped ability to analyze power or contextualize my experience left me innocently open to my white and wealthy peers. I rarely suspected that they or our teachers meant me any harm. Unlike my classmate, I wasn't thinking much about race or class. But ignorance was bliss. I had fun.

I want Is to have a power analysis as early as possible.
I also want her to have as much fun as possible at school, in
the neighborhood, away at summer camp, wherever she finds
herself. Because I want these things for my daughter, I need to
make sure she feels she belongs. I need to make sure she has
community, people with whom—not just against whom—to
define herself. When I imagine what this might look like, I
realize I want her to have a cultural home, a group in which
she feels seen and affirmed as a black girl. I also want her to
have a political home, a group in which she learns how to
make meaning, strategize, and take collective action. In an
ideal world, these groups would be one and the same.

We don't live in an ideal world, but I wonder whether it's
possible to find an ideal city, a place with more of the nanny
shares, playgrounds, and preschools that could put us in
community with like-minded peers starting now. We live in
Cincinnati, and we're here because family is here. This prox-
imity provides me with more childcare than I could afford if
we lived elsewhere. More importantly, I think it will help my
daughter feel a foundational sense of belonging. She has people. She comes from somewhere, the same place her mom and
dad come from. I grew up with this deep sense of stability
grounded in blood relations, and I think it made me more
confident in the world.

But living in southwestern Ohio has its challenges. Is and
I live a stone's throw from what was solidly Trump country
in 2016. Just beyond our barely blue county lies a sea of red.
Trump won Ohio (which had gone twice for Obama), carrying about 52 percent of the state's vote. Of the five areas

where Clinton scored a decisive victory—the counties containing Cleveland, Columbus, Cincinnati, Toledo, and Athens (a rural town that's home to Ohio University)—our county gave her the smallest lead. Clinton took roughly 53 percent of the vote here in Hamilton County, Trump 43 percent.[1] It didn't take the 2016 election to make me feel conflicted about this place. My angst over what it means to be a black woman raising a black girl here has its roots in an era that precedes Trump's election.

In 2006, when I was getting a graduate degree in journalism, I spent months researching the history of race relations in Cincinnati for a book I planned to write about my hometown. The idea was prompted by the events of 2001, when the police killing of an unarmed black nineteen-year-old named Timothy Thomas set off several days of rioting and organized protests. At the time of his death, police were pursuing Thomas because he had open warrants for nonviolent misdemeanors, almost all for tickets related to traffic violations.[2] He was the fifteenth black man killed by police in a five-year period. No white suspects were killed during that time. Thomas's death was the match that lit the powder keg, unleashing black residents' frustrations over racial profiling and state violence. Beginning April 9, 2001, phalanxes of police in riot gear attempted to keep the uprising confined to Over-the-Rhine, the then-impoverished, now-gentrified neighborhood where Thomas was killed. Eventually a boycott erected a kind of picket line around the city, with black organizers issuing a plea that entertainers and national conferences—anything that turned a blind eye to the pattern of police violence and gave Cincinnati an economic boost—stay away. It feels like ancient history now, given the national conversation about police violence against black people that gained steam in 2009 after Bay Area Rapid Transit officer Johannes Mehserle killed Oscar Grant. But at the time, Cincinnati gave the United States this century's first so-called race riot—at the time, the largest since the LA riots—and became ground zero for an urgent but fleeting conversation about police accountability and black communities.

My research five years after that conflagration revealed that race riots had been a common feature of Cincinnati life since its earliest days. But historically, the more typical occurrence had been white residents rioting against what they considered to be black interlopers—successful black entrepreneurs, laborers they believed to be displacing white workers, or black people who had moved into previously lily-white neighborhoods. In the early 1990s, when I was entering my teen years, Cincinnati drew national attention for its displays of conservatism, antiblack racism, and anti-Semitism. The Klan repeatedly staged events on Fountain Square in the heart of downtown, and reports surfaced that Reds owner Marge Schott had referred to some of the baseball team's players as "million-dollar niggers."[3]

It's not that progressive coastal cities are without such problems. It was a New York City police officer who put Eric Garner in a fatal chokehold. We watched Mehserle shoot and kill an unarmed Grant at close range on a subway platform in Oakland, California. But in addition to the dramatic moments in Cincinnati's history, there are also the little annoyances, the more subtle signs of cultural stagnancy.

First there's the saying, attributed to Mark Twain, "When the end of the world comes, I want to be in Cincinnati, because it's always twenty years behind the times." My hometown is a place where in the course of meeting each other, adults often ask, "Where'd you go to high school?" as a way to gauge someone's class, religious, and political backgrounds. There's significance in whether someone's from the east or the west side, whether they grew up in the suburbs or attended a public magnet, got a posh private school education or chose Catholic instead. Those of us who grew up here use these clues to clock someone immediately. Implicit in the question is the assumption that if you live in Cincinnati, you must be a native. Why else would you be here?

We have a legacy of protest as well. In the early 1950s, civil rights icon Marian Spencer spearheaded the legal fight to allow black people into Coney Island, a local waterpark. Spencer and the local chapter of the NAACP were also key players in the 1974 lawsuit *Mona Bronson et al. v. Board of Education of the City School District of the City of Cincinnati*, which eventually resulted in a voluntary desegregation plan for the city's schools. My middle school social studies teacher had been involved in free speech protests in 1990 when Hamilton County sheriff Simon Leis tried to have a Robert Mapplethorpe exhibit kicked out of the city's Contemporary Art Center on claims that the photographs were pornographic. Not all Cincinnatians have taken the city's trademark conservatism and oppression lying down.

If I wasn't a mom, I'd know how to go out and build community for myself. I've done it in multiple cities throughout my adult life. But I need tips on how to do it with my child. I feel too frazzled, too busy with work and domestic responsibilities to seek out new friends and allies, and now I'm looking for peers for Is as well. How do I do that here? On a warm April day, I drive into North Avondale, an enclave of Cincinnati I've idealized since my youth. In the hipster-friendly, predominately white neighborhood where we live now, we have things that North Avondale lacks: bars and restaurants, music venues, a café where I can work when I have a few hours of childcare. But North Avondale has other things I want for Is. It's integrated in terms of race and class and home to a critical mass of the city's black middle class. It's also home to one of the magnet elementary schools that adopted the Montessori pedagogy as a way to desegregate the public school system in the 1970s and '80s. Is's dad grew up in the neighborhood and attended the school.

I'm here to interview Dr. Kimya Moyo, known to many in the community and nationwide as Mama Kimya. Moyo is a Cincinnati native who moved to Chicago in the 1970s and worked closely with Haki Madhubuti, the Black Arts movement poet, educator, and a founder of Third World Press. By 1993, she was back in Cincinnati with her family, and she founded Sankofa, a youth enrichment program intended to deepen students' critical thinking skills and expose them to the history and culture of the African diaspora.[4] I attended my first Kwanzaa celebration in Moyo's home about fifteen years ago. When I ask how she identifies politically, she seems bemused by the question. "I am someone who supports people who support social justice issues across the board," she says. "The way in which I present myself is probably more African-centered than anything else." She emphasizes that that's not a political orientation. "What I try to do is just be consistent in supporting and advocating for African people and African-centered issues."

Moyo moved her family between Chicago, Cincinnati, and Liberia before settling here for good in 1984. She taught math at the local arts magnet school before becoming a district administrator. At seventy, Moyo exudes wisdom and calm. I have sought her out because it seems she figured out how to live in her hometown while staying engaged and active and exposing her children to the world beyond this city. I ask Moyo how she met the challenge of raising black children in a city where there are comparatively so few options.

"You can't say, 'It's difficult or it can't be done,'" she tells me. "You have to say, 'I'm looking for ways to do it.' If there is no museum here, 'OK, we're going to go to Chicago or Detroit or DC.' We can't allow the fact that there is not what we're looking for, that it's not here. We have to see that we can somehow get it here.' We need a black play? OK, who's doing a black play? How can I get them to Cincinnati?' And do it. Figure it out. Why? Because your children's lives are at stake."

I agree with Moyo that the stakes are high and that it's my job as a parent to support my daughter in finding meaning and a sense of pride early in life. I want her to feel that she has a right to a good life and access to the tools she needs to create it. I sometimes idealize coastal cities, but maybe the best example of what I'd like for our family is just north of here in the form of Detroit Summer. In 1992, that effort was launched by a group of Detroit organizers that included James and Grace Lee Boggs. James Boggs was the black American activist, intellectual, and former auto worker who wrote *The American Revolution: Pages from a Negro Worker's Notebook,* among other books. Grace Lee Boggs was a Chinese American philosopher and activist who inspired many political seekers and visionaries in my generation in Detroit and nationwide. Together, the Boggses were giants in left and civil rights movement organizing and thinking until James Boggs's death in 1993. Grace Lee Boggs was one hundred years old when she died in 2015. In her autobiography, *Living for Change,* she describes Detroit Summer as "an Intergenerational Multicultural Youth Program/Movement to rebuild, redefine, respirit Detroit from the Ground Up."[5] In that first incarnation, the program was comprised of annual four-week sessions that convened college-aged young people, elders, and children to work on such projects as turning empty lots into community gardens and creating public murals. In the evening, the work continued through community dinners at which participants would, in Boggs's words, "grapple with challenging questions in intergenerational dialogues or develop media or organizing skills in workshops."

In 1992, Julia Putnam was sixteen years old and the first young person to sign up for Detroit Summer. She remembers the messages she'd heard about her hometown until that point: "Black people burned down the city in '67, and you've got to go away to college to get away from all this." Detroit Summer, with its bringing together of elders and youth and

Detroiters and suburbanites and college kids from around the country, offered her for the first time "exposure to different kinds of people" and "the truth of what happened to Detroit." She learned that despite massive disinvestment and white flight, there was a history of Detroiters who stayed in their city and committed to making it vibrant. She learned that she didn't have to leave home to be successful, in part because there were others with whom she could join forces to, as she puts it, "make a way out of no way."

Putnam is now principal of a public charter school named after the Boggses. I ask how she passes on to students what she received as a participant in Detroit Summer, and she answers with an anecdote: Recently she took a group of young people to a part of the city where the so-called Detroit renaissance is on full tilt. Long-empty lots and storefronts have become home to expensive boutiques and posh restaurants offering thirty-dollar entrees and craft cocktails. One student, who is from the mostly black and low-income neighborhood surrounding the school, asked Putnam, "Are we still in Detroit?" She explained that not only was this Detroit but that these newer businesses had sprung up around a beloved twenty-year-old bakery that was inspired by the Boggses' vision for the city. It was only because of this popular, long-standing, community-oriented small business that developers wanted to be on this corner, cashing in on the cultural cachet that Avalon has built over the years, Putnam explained. "There's no sense that Detroiters created this Detroit," she says. But she's interrupting that narrative with her work, just as elder activists did for her twenty-five years ago.

After talking to Putnam and Moyo, I check my snobbery and run an inventory: What does my hometown have to offer that I can build on and share with my daughter? After all, adults in my life did that for me throughout my childhood. My mom and other family members made sure I had a range of affirming, enriching experiences. We went to most plays with a black cast that came to Playhouse in the Park. (I clearly remember all the church hats in the audience at *Mama, I Want to Sing!*) Ditto exhibitions of black art that came to the Cincinnati Art Museum or Taft Museum. Every year on Martin Luther King Day, we went to the commemorative program downtown at the majestic Music Hall. Choirs from all over the country came annually to that same venue for a concert of Negro spirituals, and that's where I first heard live performances of songs like "Ezekiel Saw the Wheel" and "Didn't My Lord Deliver Daniel?"

When I was sixteen or seventeen, I decided I wanted to study African dance and Dunham technique, the style created by dancer and anthropologist Katherine Dunham, and I studied with an encouraging veteran black teacher at the Contemporary Dance Theater. In the summer of 1997, when I was nineteen and home from college, I wandered from the downtown law firm where I worked as a receptionist into the nearby Contemporary Art Center. This was before the Zaha Hadid redesign, when it was just a few rooms overlooking the bus depot at Government Square. There I stared at silhouettes of antebellum scenes affixed to the white walls and was mesmerized by an early Kara Walker exhibit.

Exposure also came through conversation. I remember talking with Aunt Pam about South African apartheid after she saw Athol Fugard's *Master Harold and the Boys*. I remember an age-appropriate debrief after she went to see Spike Lee's original *She's Gotta Have It*. Art that was making waves nationally or globally made its way back to me through the retellings of people in my life who saw themselves as citizens of the world and wanted the same and more for me.

If Is grows up here, she will have access to literature, music, and art that makes her think. Cincinnati isn't a cultural mecca, but it's a midsized city with well-funded and well-regarded arts institutions. The people in her life will take her places. We will talk with her about what's beautiful, complex, and provocative. But my own memories center on passive pursuits, on *taking in* some aspect of culture that happened to come through town. In Putnam's telling, what has made Detroit unique in recent decades is the presence of a group of people who are committed to creating homegrown culture and taking political action together. The first step, it seems, is to find our comrades- and allies-to-be.

I'm on a work trip to Lisbon when I meet G. Rosaline Preudhomme, a seventy-three-year-old activist who's been on the front lines in battles ranging from Brooklyn Congress on Racial Equality (CORE) demonstrations to efforts to desegregate the Ocean Hill–Brownsville schools. The trip is organized by Drug Policy Alliance, a national organization I worked for just after college that advocates replacing punitive drug policies with a public health approach. I'm in Lisbon to learn how the Portuguese ended their own war on drugs in 2001 and adopted more humane interventions. Preudhomme and I talk over breakfast one morning, and like Moyo, she isn't interested in hearing me lament how hard it is to find a political or cultural home for my child and me. "You need to find what you would conceptualize as a village life," she tells me. Preudhomme, a mother of four, spent the first sixteen years of her life in Barbados in a village of around three hundred people. Those years taught her that village life is the optimal environment for a child because of the way it breaks open the narrow, inward focus of the nuclear family and gives all capable, willing adults the role of caregiver. In her community, parents saw themselves as responsible for all the children, she tells me. Growing up, she received the message, "You are being raised by a community that loves, supports, and respects you. They will hold you up." She advises me to find mentors, four or five people who can form the kernel of the village I'm creating for Is. Where do I find them? "Any kind of social setting that you find yourself in," she says, and she suggests a faith community or town hall meetings, places where "you meet people who want to advocate."

ॐ

I KNOW I'M ASKING FOR A LOT. I WANT IS TO BE COSMO-politan but rooted. I want her to be an independent, analytical thinker but to also value community. So far I have a Barbadian village and Detroit Summer as models for what I want for our family. Sometimes I think this particular quest would be easier if we moved to Oakland, where I lived for six years before returning home to Cincinnati. Is and I wouldn't have the same kind of generational attachment to the place, but we would be somewhere with a legacy of left politics and a DIY ethic where I have dear friends and ties to robust cultural institutions. It's a city with a lot of transplants who are drawn by the promise of progressive-movement jobs, mild weather, and a vibrant inclusivity created by lifelong Oaklanders.

But in the spring of 2018, just as my nostalgia for Oakland is peaking, something interesting happens. My social media feeds are filled with accounts of white people calling the police on black people who are engaged in acts that don't seem the least bit criminal, thus needlessly exposing them to surveillance and potential violence. A Yale graduate student doesn't like that her black peer is napping in a common area. She calls the police. Some young black men sitting in a Philadelphia Starbucks tell the barista they'll wait for their meeting to start before they make a purchase. She calls the police. Someone sees a black man moving into his New York City apartment and calls the police. After a dispute over plastic utensils at an Alabama Waffle House, a black woman asks for the district manager's phone number and staff calls the police, who show up and tackle her to the ground. Black people are barbecuing at Oakland's Lake Merritt—where I walked, sunned myself, and relaxed with friends almost daily during the years I lived there—and a white onlooker calls the police.

The meme resulting from the Oakland incident is hilarious and powerful. The image of the white woman in sunglasses and a blue sweatshirt, dubbed #BBQBecky, on her cell phone to Oakland police pops up everywhere. She's pho-
topped onto the Ernie Barnes painting of languid black

bodies dancing that was featured during the *Good Times* credits. She's photoshopped onto an image of Diana Ross and Michael Jackson easing on down the road as characters in *The Wiz*. She's photoshopped—this time with swimming goggles and snorkel—onto the iconic still of the characters Juan and the young Chiron sharing a quiet moment in the ocean in *Moonlight*. The message is spot on: white people are calling the police on black people for simply existing, and it's not just happening in the so-called flyover states. In an interview with NPR's *All Things Considered*, Jason Johnson, a professor of politics and journalism at Morgan State University, describes what's happening: "These people are calling the police first because they think that blacks are inherently dangerous. And they feel that the police are there to work as their personal racism valets and remove black people from the situation."[6]

This is nothing new. As with the police killings of black people that have filled our feeds for the past decade, what's new is the documentation made possible by cell phones, social media's role in disseminating that documentation, and corporate media's interest in critically covering the incidents. And what's new for me, or at least what I'm seeing differently as a mom, is that even living in a place long viewed as a progressive enclave won't save your family.

Aya de Leon, a writer and UC Berkeley professor, and her husband are raising their nine-year-old daughter in Berkeley. In talking with de Leon, I see more clearly that raising a black child in a metropolitan coastal area just brings a different set of challenges. De Leon grew up in Berkeley, the child of a blonde, light-skinned Puerto Rican mom and an African American dad. She remembers the city's schools being integrated when she was a kid in the early 1970s and the wave of gentrification that hit in the 1980s. For her own child, de Leon has never simply chosen the school closest to her home or the option that's most convenient. Instead, like me, she's viewed her family's choices about childcare and school as setting the stage for her daughter's earliest experiences of community. And race has been at the center of considerations about how to make sure the child feels that she belongs.

De Leon's daughter had been the only black child in her first preschool and was one of two at another program. But kids of color and those from multiracial families have tended to make up a sizable minority of these classrooms. The "of color" label is used a lot in progressive circles to signal racial inclusiveness. But de Leon balks at the assumption that an environment that has a lot of kids whose parents identify them as being of color is automatically good for brown-skinned black children. "When you have a three-year-old, the various multiracial Asian and Latino kids who are very light-skinned are not helping your child" develop positive self-image, she tells me.

In her younger years, de Leon explains, her daughter grappled with the prevalence of the multiracial families in her progressive preschools. "The African heritage of the blonde friend is not impacting her in the same way," she tells me. "It really was different for her to look around and not see anyone who was remotely as brown as her. At that point you could see more of the racial consciousness setting in, and it was tough on her." As she speaks, I'm reminded that I'd never fully grasped how race worked in the Bay Area. Blackness was simultaneously devalued and coveted. Black culture was placed on a pedestal, adopted by others with ease. And in some circles, racial solidarity among black people seemed out of fashion, passé. There was a postracialism to the Bay's wokeness that often struck me as simplistic. It's not until I hear de Leon explain it in the context of her daughter's school communities that I realize that as an adult, I observed that aspect of the culture with curiosity. As the mother of a black girl with two brown-skinned black parents, it would frustrate me.

When it came time for her daughter to enter grade school, de Leon peered into the future to imagine how she might turn out as an older child. She wondered whether she should keep seeking out experimental private schools with an emphasis on social-emotional learning even if it meant there'd be just a few black kids. Berkeley's public schools, which she says have become "too white for me to feel confident in sending my kid there," weren't appealing, at least not while her child was so young. Eventually she chose a predominately black and Latino public charter school in Oakland's Fruitvale area, a historically Latino neighborhood that's a twenty- to thirty-minute commute from the family's northwest Berkeley home. She describes it as a school with a social justice focus that was created for kids of color by educators of color.

By this stage in her child's education, de Leon was clear: she didn't want her child to be what she calls "the raisin in the oatmeal." She wanted black and brown friends for her daughter, and prioritizing that would mean choosing a school with

lots of black and brown kids. Based on the connections the
girl had made in preschool, de Leon says,

> She was being sort of set up to be the cool black friend. She
> would probably be put on a track from elementary school
> to high school of having mixed groups of friends, and she
> was set up to be the black friend. I was confident that all of
> those girls would be great girls. But there would be some
> piece there about her always being the darkest one, always
> being the one with the kinkiest hair. I didn't want her to
> be tracked that way. I wanted her to be in an environment
> where she was just going to have to figure out her relation-
> ship to brown girls.

De Leon agrees that much of the work she's putting in now is
in anticipation of her daughter's teenage years. "From the time
she was little, I've been building up the black girl friend crew,"
she tells me. "I'm very intentional about the friendships that I
nurture. Going into the tween years, the beauty stuff is gonna
hit hard. And when it does, I just need her to have brown girls
around her."

Beginning in the 1990s, a body of research has shown
that black girls navigate the teen years better than girls of
other races and better than black boys as well. Black girls
come through adolescence less scathed by the onslaught of
messages that they don't measure up to mainstream standards of desirability and success. One early study found that
black girls fare better precisely because they look to their
families and communities for affirmation rather than to

teachers or the school system.[7] This is yet another reason to make sure those communities are filled with black women and girls who can assure them that most problems come from how the world views them, not from some inherent deficiency.

I want Is to have her blackness affirmed, but I want something else for her, too: a sense of political or intellectual belonging. For me, this hasn't only come through association with other black people or even other people of color. When I have a thorny question about journalistic ethics, I turn to Kristina, an education reporter who was born in Latvia and who keeps respect for sources and kindness at the center of her work. Jaime is a white social worker whose parents were in the Communist Party. Her dad, whom I met at a lefty writers' retreat in Vermont a decade ago, saw in us kindred spirits and set us up. I am in daily contact with Jodie, a white Canadian whose work involves getting American social justice organizers in tough conversations about the future of their movements. I reflect on and muddle through parenting, Buddhist practice, and the writing life with Elizabeth, another white Canadian with roots in Colombia. Dean, my high school English teacher, once helped me get a great job teaching social studies and now leads the integrated Montessori high school where I worked. She's a white principal obsessed with recruiting more teachers of color and with getting white teachers to recognize and root out their unconscious biases. Kat and I met our first year in college and have been talking journalism, politics, and life ever since. Her grandfather was a founder of American studies, but she never mentioned that. I learned about his role in the history of American thought while reading a biography of Ralph Ellison.

The white friends I have made since leaving high school are, for the most part, either red diaper babies or not from the United States. We talk about race explicitly and often. If we couldn't do that, we wouldn't be friends. De Leon's choices about school environment make sense to me, but I don't necessarily have fixed ideas about what the racial makeup of Is's community should be. I need for the unifying principle to be a politic more than I need for it to be a racial identity. I think I want for her what Julia Putnam had decades ago, which is a lot like what writer, filmmaker, and activist dream hampton had more recently for her daughter, Nina.

In 2007, hampton returned to her midwestern hometown after two decades in New York City. She wanted a different pace for her daughter, then twelve, who was already being sexually harassed by grown men on the street. Stop and frisk was common practice in New York, and Nina was witnessing daily police harassment of black and brown bodies in their neighborhood. Detroit, with its car culture and family available to help with childcare, beckoned. Back home, hampton enrolled her daughter in school in wealthy, suburban Grosse Pointe, where she could get the quality of education she'd received at her exclusive New York private school. "I didn't have faith in Detroit Public Schools anymore," says hampton, herself a DPS alumna. "I knew about the divestment that had been happening." Her academics were in place, but what was missing were the cultural and political spaces Nina had become accustomed to back east. There had been a rites-of-passage program in Brooklyn, Dance Africa at the Brooklyn Academy of Music, and the annual African Street Festival at Boys and Girls High School. Hampton had been a founding member of the New York chapter of the Malcolm X Grassroots Movement. "Nina would be at whatever we were doing," she remembers. "I took her to rallies. I took her to meetings."

But in Detroit, she was no longer swimming in black culture and liberation politics. Hampton had to put effort into making sure Nina had a social circle beyond largely white, provincial Grosse Pointe. "I was looking to balance that out in a really intentional way," hampton remembers. "And then that all came together like magic."

Just as the family returned, a group of young people was working to revive Detroit Summer, which had been struggling financially. Hampton had a friend who'd told her, "You have got to meet Invincible," the Detroit-based rapper also known as ill Weaver who was part of a group reconvening the project. Hampton and her daughter ran into Weaver one day at the city's farmers' market, and Weaver invited Nina to join Detroit Summer. Hampton was struck by how seriously Weaver and the other facilitators—people in their twenties and thirties—took their role as adult allies. They saw youth in their preteens as ready and able to take on real responsibilities and leadership.

In 2010, the US Social Forum came to Detroit, and Nina spent her first weeks as part of the Detroit Summer reboot. "Nina and these amazing kids from Detroit, there were about ten or twelve of them, wheatpasted the city," hampton remembers. "They did this whole multimedia project where they interviewed community leaders"—people like Boggs and members of the city's Food Justice Task Force and Coalition Against Police Brutality—"and from these interviews they created this number that you could dial in to listen to snippets of it." They made a photo collage, joined the US Social Forum's opening march down Woodward Avenue, and attended the Allied Media Conference, hosted annually in Detroit, as a group. Most importantly, hampton says, Nina "made lifelong friends, which is what I'd hoped for."

It wasn't all perfect, she says and laughs. "I told ill, 'If you put my kid in another four-hour meeting, she's gonna hate organizing.'" It's true. There's an art to teaching young people the skills they need to engage in political change without boring them or turning them off, and I know the leaders of Detroit Summer didn't have it all figured out. But I'm struck by this reflection from Tracey Hollins, who at fifteen got involved in the first iteration of the program in 1992, just as Putnam had. "It filled your head with answers to questions you'd had all of your life and questions that no one can answer," Hollins said.[8]

I want this kind of perspective-broadening experience for Is. I want her to learn early how to engage in civil but fierce political debate, a skill I didn't acquire until I moved to New York for college. I remember being shocked by how my classmates and friends and the adults I encountered talked to each other, how there was no place for the careful politeness that had governed and neutralized so many interactions back home. I want her to learn skills like wheatpasting and interviewing and to do it alongside other young people who are excited about the political content of the projects. And talking to hampton and Putnam makes me feel that it's possible to find both a political and cultural home for my daughter here in the Midwest.

Cincinnati isn't Detroit. We never had the scale of opportunities that pulled so many southern black workers north and into the auto factories. We lack the radical history, the legacy of black, left formations like the Detroit Revolutionary Union Movement (DRUM). We don't have Motown (though we did have King Records), and we're not a birthplace of house music (though there's lots of good bluegrass). What we lack most, vis-á-vis my quest for belonging, is that constant building and nurturing of community that I feel every time I visit Detroit, which I do often as someone who's been involved as a board member and participant in the Allied Media Conference since it moved there two decades ago. Weaver and hampton and Nandi Comer and Jenny Lee and Mike Medow and adrienne maree brown and Morgan Willis and Diana Nucera and many others make these Detroit institutions happen, and they are part of my political family. When I spend time with them, I wonder if I can take the advice of Moyo and Preudhomme and build a similar village back home.

The mandate is a compelling one. Places like the Bay or New York aren't perfect, as de Leon's experience shows. And I've always been a little frustrated by the ease with which some coastal folks dismiss the rest of the country and express shock that anyone would choose to live here. When I moved to New York for college, someone asked me with a straight face if I'd driven a tractor to school, and people had no shame admitting they couldn't tell Cincinnati from St. Louis on a map. Throughout my adulthood, I've experienced big city residents' arrogant pride in their own ignorance. This ignorance has broader implications, of course. After the 2016 election, we had to withstand news story after news story that told us that the center of the country was populated only by the white working class, as if no people of color live in the Midwest or are blue collar.

Maybe in finding our village, Is and I can help create something irresistible in the heartland, something that's for our own benefit and makes life here vibrant and full of possibility. I don't have to look just east or west for a model of how that's done. I can also look north to Detroit. What matters is that I help my daughter learn how to live with dignity and self-love and that I surround her with a team that supports her and that she can support. I want her to learn early on what it means to act in solidarity. I want her to be lighthearted, and I think this will be easier if she knows she doesn't have to bear the weight of the world alone.

CHAPTER 6

School

It's a weekday morning, and I'm reverse commuting, driving from our apartment about five minutes northwest of downtown Cincinnati to my mom's house in the suburbs, where I often go to work. I'm listening to a podcast called *Why Is This Happening?*, and Chris Hayes is interviewing Nikole Hannah-Jones, the MacArthur genius and *New York Times Magazine* staffer whose education reporting informs a lot of my thinking on schools.

Early in the episode, Hannah-Jones makes a claim I've never heard put so clearly: all of our conversations about how to fix the so-called achievement gap, the phrase used to describe certain groups of kids' lower scores on standardized tests, start from accepting that US schools will be segregated. It's as if we've given up on any presumption that our children will attend integrated schools. Instead, we are starting with a yawning gap as a given and trying to work from there. Few people talk about desegregation as a goal for education policy. Instead, the focus is as follows: Given that poor black and brown kids go to these schools and white kids of all classes go to these other schools over here, what can we do to make sure all kids are scoring similarly on these tests, which are often held up as the primary way to measure learning? In other words, how can we make separate equal?

I taught social studies for two years, from 2003 to 2005, in a Cincinnati public high school. I covered education for two years, from 2006 to 2008, for the *Milwaukee Journal Sentinel*, and I still occasionally report on schools. In my personal and professional lives, I've seen with my own eyes that segregated schools are the norm, but until I started thinking about what kind of education I want for Is, I never realized how obfuscating all the "achievement gap" conversations truly are. This morning, as I listen to the podcast, I remember that I have access to something most black Americans don't: an address that would put my child into one of the country's wealthiest school districts. Two sick, accepted realities in this country are that the quality of a child's schooling depends on where she lives and that educational resources are concentrated where white children are.[1]

At some point before Is turns five, should we move back to my childhood home so she can have a free, well-resourced education alongside some of the metro area's most privileged kids? How much do I care about things like test scores anyway, and should I instead prioritize a K–12 education that will put us in community with a mostly black or racially inclusive group of people who we're genuinely excited to learn and play with? I drive north and my mind races. I spent my kindergarten through senior years in that exclusive, high-performing district, as did my mother. I'm not sure I want the same for my child.

I grew up in the 1980s and 1990s in a small community of about three hundred people called Camp Dennison. It was a paper mill town in the early nineteenth century. In the 1840s it was first connected to Cincinnati by railroad, the traces of which marked a boundary I couldn't ride my bike beyond as a young child. The dirt path we used to call "the tracks" have since been paved and turned into a bike trail that ushers weekend warriors along seventy miles of scenic southwestern Ohio. During the Civil War, a large swath of land in the area was a training camp for Union soldiers, giving the neighborhood its current name. Camp Dennison has been integrated and home to a sizable black middle class since the late nineteenth century. In 1933, my twelve-year-old maternal grandfather moved with his sister and their maternal grandparents from their nearby farm into the neighborhood to be close to extended family. Those great-great-grandparents built the house where I grew up.

That house happens to be less than a mile outside Indian Hill, the wealthiest neighborhood in the greater Cincinnati area and the twelfth richest in the country, with an average household income of around $314,000 in 2016.[2] A drive through Indian Hill takes you past multimillion-dollar homes and street signs warning drivers to steer clear of equestrians. These two communities share a school district, and so I learned alongside the children of executives at Procter & Gamble, Chiquita, and Cincinnati's other Fortune 500 companies. My classmates' parents—their dads mostly—were highly paid lawyers and doctors. From ages five to eighteen, I spent time at soccer games, at birthday parties, and on vacation with the children of the city's captains of industry. I got to see their wealth and tremendous political power up close. At their sprawling homes I might glimpse a photograph of a smiling father with his arm around the shoulder of George H. W. Bush or an impeccably dressed mother ordering about the team of gardeners charged with manicuring the surrounding acres. On vacation with my best friend, whose family owned a small island off the coast of Maine, I learned to distinguish between "starboard" and "port" while navigating Penobscot Bay on their forty-five-foot sailboat. When I was seventeen years old, this same friend's father secured a summer job for me as a receptionist at the downtown law firm where he was a partner, and there I saw how major decisions affecting the city were made and who participated in making them.

We weren't wealthy. My mom had a solid job in retail as a merchandise planner for most of my childhood. Elders in my family had worked in Indian Hill homes—my great-grandmother as a maid, my grandmother as a caterer, and my grandfather as a sometime bartender or valet for their lavish parties. My grandfather's full-time job for decades had been at the gravel pit in Camp Dennison, where he'd operated large machinery to extract rounded stones deposited by the Little Miami River. We were a middle-class family back when that still felt attainable.

In my school community, I never had the sense that white parents didn't want me around. For the most part, I felt welcome. But I was also aware that I and other black kids at the school (most of whom came from Camp Dennison) were in the distinct minority. Whiteness and wealth were the norm, and we posed no threat to the established order. All of the authority figures in the buildings and on the playgrounds where we spent our time were white. I never had a nonwhite teacher or administrator until I reached college. I will never forget the day Peter Johnson, a legendary black admissions officer from Columbia University, showed up at my high school to recruit. He blew in there in his sharply tailored suit and his tales of campus life and changed me. From that day until I showed up on campus in the summer of 1996, I dreamed of going to Columbia.

I went through a stage in my college years and early twenties when I resented the slights and microaggressions I sometimes had to endure as a student at Indian Hill's schools. Now I look back on those years in awe that an accident of geography—my ancestors' choice to make home in that particular semirural suburb of Cincinnati—exposed me to something black children aren't supposed to see in this country. We're not supposed to see that we're just as smart as white kids. We're not supposed to see that even if our families aren't as wealthy, we deserve to be in the same spaces as white kids and we can excel once we're there. I graduated high school with a GPA over 4.0 and a string of 4s and 5s on Advanced Placement tests, including Latin, English Literature, and Calculus. I went on to graduate magna cum laude and Phi Beta Kappa from an Ivy League school and then get a master's degree from that same institution. But today's conversation about schools will tell you black kids cognitively just can't cut it. Today's conversation about schools will tell you it's not the lack of access to challenging curriculum or the shoddy materials or the rampant disorganization holding black children back from thriving academically; it's the kids themselves. The truth is the schools we're concentrated in can't cut it, and there's little public will to do anything about it.

Expensive homes clustered in a neighborhood create a sizable tax base from which to fund local public schools. Racism and poverty have historically kept black people out of such neighborhoods, leaving us in underresourced schools where that much-discussed achievement gap persists. Research shows that a child can grow up in a home with highly educated parents who have good jobs, and that child is unlikely to move up the income ladder if the home is located in a poor neighborhood. This is of particular importance for black families, who tend to stay in high-poverty neighborhoods even as they move up the class ladder. According to a recent Economic Mobility Project report, "Even if blacks are able to make gains in economic or social status in one generation, they often remain in social environments that are disadvantaged across multiple dimensions, and that may make it more difficult to transmit advantages to the next generation."[3]

Even though I have two fancy degrees and a fairly good income, I know my toehold in the middle class is precarious. Downward mobility is common for black people, and I worry that living in a mixed- or low-income community means I'm more likely to lose any gains in economic or social status my family has made. Sure, the city lover in me prefers the neighborhood where Is and I now live. It's weird and fun and walkable. It feels safer, more welcoming for a family like ours. The neighborhood where I grew up has become increasingly white in the past couple of decades and went for Trump in 2016. And in neighboring Indian Hill, 65 percent voted for Trump.[4] It's not exactly home to the white working class. But how much does that really matter? Why wouldn't I move into a posh suburban school district if it costs me next to nothing and if the data tell me it could mean a world of difference for my daughter?

Because, as Aya de Leon tells me, conversations about black kids and schools focus too much on the academic harms endured by kids who don't go to high-performing, majority-white schools. What's overlooked are the psychic and cultural harms that these so-called good schools inflict. De Leon directs Poetry for the People, an arts and activism program that's part of UC Berkeley's African American Studies Department. She says the high schools her black students come from offer a clear indication of the types of burdens they're carrying. "If you're in a hood school, the harms are clear, and you know when they're happening that you're being harmed," she says, and lists fights and subpar academic offerings among such violations. "In these white environments, you're being harmed, and you don't even know it because you think there is something wrong with you. [You think] if only you could get these white people to like you," then everything would be OK. "This is a different type of harm, and it's a stealth harm, and you internalize it really deeply."

I hear something similar from Monifa Bandele, a Brooklyn-based mother and organizer who is a senior vice president with the advocacy organization MomsRising.org. Her teenaged girls have gone to Brooklyn Friends, a private Quaker school, since middle school. Before that, they went to what she describes as black-led Christian private schools. Her concern with these earlier environments was the focus on discipline. She realized at one point that her then fifth grader was afraid of her math teacher and would become visibly uncomfortable when the woman walked close to her desk. "That's not what school is supposed to be," Bandele says.

Bandele was drawn to the Quaker school because she identified with the focus on social justice and appreciated the leaders' willingness to engage students in the issues of the day. For example, students attended a rally after police killed Michael Brown in Ferguson and then had a facilitated discussion to process the experience. But in addition to values aligned with what Bandele teaches at home, the school has exposed her girls to what she describes as a white liberal racism they've had to learn how to navigate. Her daughters, now sixteen and nineteen, have responded in different ways. Because of their high levels of awareness around issues of race and power, they see both the intentional and unintentional racism at school. Bandele has worried that their sharp perception has left them at times exhausted by the work of dealing with outright aggression and microaggressions, but she's also seen them take it in stride. "I can check you on this; then we can still work on the science project together," she tells me, giving an example of how one girl has responded. "You shouldn't touch her hair, and let's get these projects done."

"We have no options as black mothers. Either you put your kids in a racially hostile environment, or you put your kids in a quote-unquote bad school," Bandele says. "Where all the kids are black, there's trauma. Where all the kids are white, there's trauma. There's not a lot of in-between."

The pressures can be a lot for parents. De Leon remembers her daughter testing below grade level in reading while attending a total Spanish-language immersion program. De Leon was nervous at first, but the experience clarified her goals for her daughter's education. She decided she didn't care about the overly emphasized standardized tests or the drills and rote memorization it takes to score well on them. She also decided that the academic benefits of a school can't be separated from the social, cultural, and emotional benefits. "Parents are really taught to internalize whatever that score is," she tells me. "I trust the brains of young people to be curious about the world and want to learn."

Such trust in our children's innate ability to grow intellectually is remarkable, as is some parents' trust that they or their communities will be able to fill in the inevitable gaps in their children's school experiences. On that Chris Hayes podcast, Hannah-Jones discusses the impact of having chosen an underresourced school for her own daughter: "Having all-black environments means those schools and environments will be starved of resources, as they have been in every community in our country. My daughter is in an all-black school because I chose it, and culturally, it is amazing for her. Educationally, it is a bit of a sacrifice. It just is."[5]

I admire the choices that Hannah-Jones and de Leon are making—choosing the possible academic harm over the psychic harm—but I'm more likely to land where Bandele's family has. I think I can find and create experiences outside of school to help Is understand who she is as a black girl and as someone who cares about engaging meaningfully with the world. I'm not sure I will have the time to fill in major academic gaps or the money to rally a team of tutors to do it for us.

Whether Is is in school in the suburbs or a city, I know I'll also be interfacing with white parents, and I need to know how they think about race when choosing schools for their children. I assume that if I enroll Is in the suburban district I attended, these interactions will mostly consist of polite, limited small talk, requisite logistical exchanges as we set up play dates and carpools for extracurriculars. I need to decide how important it is to feel that I can have more substantive relationships with the families of my daughter's schoolmates. A handful of progressive white mothers are writing honestly about race and schools. Eula Biss has talked about the racial inequity she sees within the integrated Evanston, Illinois, school district that her son attends, and she's written about trying to set the historical record straight with her five-year-old so that he understands what it means to be white in this country.[6] Courtney Martin and Twilight Greenaway have written about searching for preschool and kindergarten programs in Oakland, a city lauded for its racial and ethnic diversity but where white parents cluster their kids into predominately white schools.[7] In 2016, while hunting for an early-childhood program for her daughter, Martin wrote:

I have never felt like such a white parent as I did on pre-school tours, surrounded by all of these other mostly middle- and upper-middle-class white and Asian people in their 30s, asking what so often felt like comically specific and sophisticated questions about little people who don't even wipe their own butts yet: What sort of exposure will my child get to math, science, and engineering? What's your philosophy regarding introverted vs. extroverted leadership development? Are packaged foods allowed? It's not that I don't want the best for my kid. It's that I don't want to be part of a system that makes "what's best" a privilege, only accessible by people who already have the time, money, and know-how to provide their kids with educational enrichment.[8]

Even choosing to live in racially diverse cities with school-aged kids makes these women the exception to the rule. For the most part, white families choose to live in predominately white neighborhoods where it's a given that they'll send their kids to predominately white schools. A recent University of Southern California study analyzed 2000 and 2010 Census data in one hundred cities to find that while racial segregation in neighborhoods has declined since the 1970s, it's declined more slowly among families with children.[9]

Even when black students make their way into well-resourced suburban schools, as I did, their experiences often diverge from that of white students. Sociologist R. L'Heureux Lewis-McCoy uses the phrase "opportunity hoarding" to describe what he saw while studying integrated suburban schools for his book *Inequality in the Promised Land: Race, Resources, and Suburban Schooling*: "I found middle class and affluent white families organizing to limit access, taking the good teachers, in the principal's office daily advocating that 'my kid gets the good programs.'"[10] As a mom, affluent or otherwise, I'd bristle at someone telling me I shouldn't advocate for my kid in the principal's office or elsewhere, but Lewis-McCoy says we should understand ways in which privilege breeds privilege. "Because families who had the most advantages often get their requests granted, they rarely think about the collateral consequences on less well-resourced families," he told an interviewer in 2014.[11]

My own mother's approach was to simply make the same kinds of demands wealthy white parents make for their kids. I tested into gifted programming early in my education. I don't take this for granted. Teachers' subjective decision making around who gets services disadvantages black and brown students. According to a 2016 study, black and Latino third graders are about half as likely as whites to be included in gifted programs.[12] During middle school I wasn't placed in a top-level math class, and I also wasn't invited to join an enrichment class for kids identified as gifted. My mom got on the phone or scheduled a meeting; changes were made; I got into those classes and did just fine. My family took an individualist approach to pushing back on decisions made at school that adversely affected me. But simply making a nuisance of oneself doesn't work for the majority of black parents, whose kids are in underresourced schools unaccustomed to bending over backward to accommodate families' requests.

Jessica Black is mom to eighteen-year-old Lavalle and thirteen-year-old Lanyiah. She's also an organizer with the Black Organizing Project in Oakland, where she offers peer-to-peer support to other black parents caught in disputes with their children's schools. I spent an afternoon with her on a hot day in July. She had walked me through her house, past the living room where she was putting party favors together for her upcoming wedding and into a backyard where the family spends a lot of time. Home gym equipment covered part of the lawn, and a tent provided shade from the eighty-five-degree heat. We settled beneath it at a table where her son had left his chess board set up, and there she told me of her own battles with her children's high-poverty schools and how she's used those experiences to inform her work with other parents.

Black leads campaigns throughout California to end the school-to-prison pipeline, the term used to describe the practices and policies that push children out of the classroom, usually by overdisciplining and undereducating them. Unprepared for higher education or meaningful employment, these young people are put on a path toward incarceration or chronic unemployment.[13] Black students are more than three times as likely as their white peers to be expelled or suspended. By selectively enforcing discipline policies and punishing such behaviors as "willful defiance," a highly subjective but commonly used reason for suspension, school staffs end up criminalizing black students through referrals to law enforcement. Fanna Gamal, an education and juvenile defense attorney who works with Black, told me the young people she works with are often heavily surveilled and policed: A child who lives in public housing walks out her front door in the morning and encounters Oakland Housing Authority police. On the way to school, she can come in contact with Bay Area Rapid Transit (BART) and city police. At school, there's the chance of a run-in with an officer on Oakland Unified School District's force. "There's really no place in your life where you're not interfacing with the cops," Gamal says.

Black says conversations about the school-to-prison pipeline typically focus on youth and teachers while leaving out equally important players: the students' families. "While that youth is getting suspended, that parent is going up to the school. That parent is sitting in those meetings. That parent is trying to figure out how to advocate for their child. That parent is sitting there listening to these people tell them how horrible their child is, which is a reflection of them. It affects the whole family unit and then has a negative impact on our community. Because now everybody's stressed out, everybody's angry," she says.

Black isn't just talking about the families she organizes. She's experienced the stress and the anger firsthand for years. It started when her son was three and in a pre-K program in Minnesota, where the family lived before moving west. She recalls being in her early twenties and sitting at a table surrounded by white school staffers. (She remembers that there was one other black person present, a speech pathologist.) She was told that her son's attention span was too short, that he foamed at the mouth, that he needed medication and an individualized education program, or IEP. Black recalls being a young mother and feeling like she didn't know much at the time, but the Lavalle she knew and loved wasn't the Lavalle these people were describing. She refused to sign the document allowing the school to start special education services. "I was like, 'I won't be signing anything,'" she remembers. "I just felt like it wasn't right."

Research has shown that black children are often under-identified or misidentified for special education services and that providing students with adequate support depends on solid communication and trust between the parent and the school. Black didn't feel comfortable with these educators, which sheds some light on why she rejected the recommended services altogether.[14]

That turned out to be the first of many occasions when Black would follow her instincts when it comes to her kids' education, even if it meant rejecting whatever advice or directive she was getting from a school official. Five years ago, Black moved her children from Minnesota to Pittsburg, California, thirty miles northeast of Oakland. The surrounding school district is high-poverty, with nearly three-quarters of students receiving free or reduced-price lunches. Nearly a third of students there are English-language learners. When Black found out her son was failing math, she says she dug into the data and found that almost all of the black students at his predominately black and Latino high school were as well. Taken as a whole, black eleventh graders at the school fall well below grade-level proficiency on the state's standardized math test, according to California Department of Education data.[15] "That tells you there's something wrong with your teachers. There's something wrong with the curriculum and the methodology behind what you're teaching," she says, recalling her subsequent conversation with the school.

Black was also told that Lavalle's behavior was out of line. He wouldn't take his hoodie off in class. He had raised his voice. (In Black's eyes, her son is passionate, and his voice reflects that. His teachers' tone policing was part of the school's efforts to demasculinize him, she says.) "Teachers would complain because he wouldn't socialize, and it's like, 'Why are you complaining? He's doing what he needs to do.'"

Things haven't been any easier with her daughter. This past school year, Lanyiah was suspended for a total of twenty-six days. Her first suspension came in third grade, the first year the family was in the district. Black remembers that the removal from class came after a white boy spit on her daughter, who in turn threw an apple at him. "I've had problems ever since we got here," Black says. "This school district, all they know is to suspend her." Black eventually requested an IEP for her daughter, not because she suspected a learning disability but because she thought that would be one way to legally force the district to keep Lanyiah in school. Black says that throughout her family's time in the district, she's seen school officials abdicate responsibility again and again. "They make you feel like you are a bad parent," she tells me. "Nine out of ten of the things that happen in the school have nothing to do with how you parent your child. It's a totally different environment, a totally different culture."

I ask Black if she thinks the problems her family has experienced are racially motivated. In the United States, teachers are disproportionally female (75 percent) and white

(83 percent), according to federal data. There's also evidence that students of color are often unfairly penalized when graded by white teachers—but teachers of color don't appear to exhibit this same grading bias against white children.[16] Are Black's kids suffering because white teachers and administrators are misinterpreting her children's actions or treating them unfairly?

Yes and no, she says. The staffer's race can play a role, but it's not the only thing that determines whether someone values black children. "We have people in here who want to teach our kids, but they're scared of them. They don't even see our children as children. I always had to fight for people to just realize that he [her son] was human, let alone a child."

I hear this concern from other parents as well. Bandele, the Brooklyn-based mother of two teenaged girls, recounts a disturbing incident that happened a couple of months into her older daughter's second-grade year at a charter school staffed mostly by white teachers and administrators, many of whom had gone through Teach for America, the program that offers a summer of training before placing recent college graduates in high-poverty schools for a two-year commitment. Bandele picked her daughter up one afternoon, and the girl burst into tears about a block away from the school. She'd been pushed down a flight of stairs that day, she told her mother. At first, Bandele was confused. She had just talked with her daughter's teacher, and nothing had come up. She turned back around and checked back in with the teacher, who confirmed that this had happened, but that when asked whether she was OK, the seven-year-old had said yes. "I don't believe that if a seven-year-old white girl went flying down a flight of steps you'd think that she was OK," Bandele remembers thinking. They never went back. Bandele homeschooled the girl for the rest of the year.

In my own schooling, I mostly had good experiences with my white teachers. There were a handful who I deeply admired, who fed my desire to learn, and who I felt genuinely cared about me and my development. But as a parent, I see that one bad teacher lurking around every corner. I worry about putting Is in a classroom with someone who can't see her humanity and who won't think twice about crushing her spirit. So far, I've exclusively hired people of color to care for her, mostly black women. Will I try to carry this practice into her preschool years and beyond?

Finding black educators doesn't guarantee a good experience, Black reminds me. One of the school officials who has been hardest on her daughter is a black woman. "It reminds me of how old folks would gear you up to be in line when you see white people," Black says of the way this administrator interacted with the girl. "She's gotta be able to act a certain way around the good white people. Because if you raise your voice or you use your hands to talk, then those good white people are gonna think that you're trying to be aggressive. And that's what I hear about my daughter: 'She's aggressive.' She's not aggressive. She's clear. She's very intelligent. She's direct. She's not gonna say things to you to make you feel comfortable. She's gonna say exactly what she sees and what it is."

As Black sees it, the problem isn't just the prevalence of white teachers and administrators. It's also a problem that respectability and obedience are the guiding ethic at most schools. Black's kids have grown up with a mother who's a social justice organizer and who has instilled in them a race and power analysis since they were small. That has made them a target at school. I ask Black if she regrets politicizing her kids at home given what that's meant for them at school. She doesn't hesitate: No. Her daughter might have to live through a few more terrible years of schooling, but "she's been rooted and grounded in cultural ways of knowing and being. She knows who she is," Black says. "If I think about her in the next fifteen years? Power."

Black argues that we shouldn't force our kids to hide their true selves at school. Instead, we need more school leaders who have a race analysis and carry social justice values into the classroom. Black has seen what this can look like. Her son's experience at Ralph J. Bunche Academy in Oakland has been the one bright spot in an otherwise dreary set of educational experiences, and she credits that school's principal, a black career educator named Betsye Steele. Steele used restorative justice to create a vibrant culture at the school, and Black remembers circling up for conversations where students and parents could talk honestly about problems, conflicts, and needs.[17] Steele made it clear that students were her priority. "You could be in the office, but if a student walked in there? 'I need you to hold on. Let me talk to this baby,'" Black remembers.

The leadership of a principal is key to creating a culture that works, and so is having teachers who buy into that vision. Black remembers that the staff at Ralph Bunche were predominately people of color and, as she puts it, "real people. They weren't stuck in academia." She saw teachers who set up interactive learning environments rather than rely too heavily on lecturing. She saw teachers who would let a student wear earbuds in class if it wasn't distracting other students and the work was getting done. The message was less about power struggles and control and more about making sure kids were learning and everyone felt respected.

It's refreshing to hear Black talk about a school that actually met her family's needs, and I'm struck by the deep admiration and respect with which she talks about Steele. It's a rare moment during these conversations when a mother isn't talking about making do with the lesser of two evils or the devil they know. I'd like this for us, a school environment that we actually feel excited about rather than scared into. I look around the country for other examples of unique school environments, places where parents don't have to fight so hard, places parents can trust with their children. I find a handful of schools that are led by black mothers who are themselves grappling with the concerns raised by such women as Black, Bandele, and de Leon.

જી

THE JAMES AND GRACE LEE BOGGS SCHOOL OPENED IN Detroit in 2013 as a public charter elementary school. It now serves 136 kids in kindergarten through eighth grades. Julia Putnam is a cofounder of the school and its principal. Like Steele in Oakland, she leads a school that's located in a predominately black, low-income neighborhood. She tells me the school's demographics are roughly 75 percent black, 10 percent multiracial, 10 percent white, and 5 percent Hispanic or Asian. When it opened, 85 percent of kids received a free or reduced-price lunch. That's fluctuated and now the school serves a mix of families, including those from the surrounding neighborhood and those politically aligned with the work of the Boggses, after whom the school is named.

The Boggses' philosophies guide the school. Putnam's staff uses a place-based curriculum that encourages students to feel rooted in and in service to Detroit communities. Students identify as "solutionaries" who are capable of addressing the crises they see unfolding around them. Staff emphasize certain values to the young people—so-called habits of heart, mind, and hand that Putnam says "we must cultivate in ourselves in order to be our most human human being." These include empathy, inclusion, resourcefulness, critical thinking, and self-determination and are introduced through lessons at age-appropriate intervals.

Putnam's eleven-year-old daughter attends the school. (Her thirteen-year-old son attends the private Waldorf school where he was enrolled before the Boggs School opened.) In her daughter and her classmates, Putnam sees children who "feel that their voice is respected. They have a say in things that they wouldn't have at other schools," she tells me. "They ask questions: 'Why do we do this? Why do we do it this way?'"

At two, Is is already full of questions, and I love that at a school like this one her curiosity would be encouraged rather than seen as annoying or disrespectful. This seems like a place where I would find a vibrant community of peers, too. Putnam hosts a monthly coffee talk with parents. Potlucks are common, and what's typically called the Parent Teacher Association or PTA at other schools is called the Family Action Committee at the Boggs School. Putnam tells me that the group tries to answer the question, "How do we take action to help each other?"

One example of how this ethic of support looks in practice: the school starts at 9:00 a.m. and doesn't offer care before classes start. This would have been a problem for parents who have to be at work earlier, but other parents stepped in and offered to come to school before nine o'clock and supervise while their kids played together. Families came up with this solution, Putnam tells me.

Putnam and Marisol Teachworth, the school's programming director and also a cofounder, participated in Detroit Summer together under the leadership of the Boggses. Putnam said they'll often watch parents supporting each other and feel that the spirit of Detroit Summer pervades the school. "I feel like Jimmy and Grace are looking down like, 'Yes! That!'" Putnam says.

The school has its fair share of problems, she tells me. They often use restorative justice principles to deal with conflict. Last year she and Teachworth organized a restorative justice circle with students and parents after a Spanish teacher walked out of a classroom and left the school in tears. The students had started responding to the prompts she gave in Spanish with gibberish. At first Putnam and Teachworth, who is of Puerto Rican descent, were devastated. "How did we create a school where this could happen? What are we not doing right?" Putnam remembers thinking. The next day, students circled up with school staff and their families and responded to the following questions: What happened? What did you think while it was happening? What are you thinking now?

Students admitted that they hadn't known what to do as the situation spiraled out of control. A Spanish-speaking mom shared that people had made fun of her accent growing up and that she was heartbroken that her own daughter hadn't intervened. A black mother said that while she'd always taught her son to be proud of his own heritage, the incident made her realize she hadn't taught him enough about respect for others' backgrounds. The group talked through how to best apologize to the Spanish teacher, and the discussion led not to harsh discipline for the students but to real learning and a strengthening of the school community.

A majority of the school's teaching staff is white. There are six classroom teachers, five of whom are white women. One teacher is Filipina, and lots of black adults round out the staff, serving in such roles as special education teacher, mental health support, classroom aides, and office administrator. Students often clamor for more black teachers, Putnam tells me, and her white teachers don't take offense at this. Instead, they themselves advocate for finding black teachers, make a point of bringing black parents and volunteers into the classroom, and talk explicitly with students about identity and privilege.

Putnam says it would be irresponsible to expose the students to white educators who are uncomfortable talking about race. Years ago, she was advised by the historian and civil rights activist Vincent Harding, who was black, to always ask prospective white teachers about race. His suggestion was to frame the question as, "When did you realize race was an issue in this country?"

"I'm not looking for the right answer," Putnam says. "I'm looking for how comfortable people feel answering." Here Putnam echoes something I learned from Monique Morris, an expert on the criminalization of black girls in schools. When I interviewed her in 2014, Morris emphasized that a teacher's race or ethnicity alone doesn't determine whether she'll be able to build successful relationships with students of color. At the time, Morris had recently finished focus groups in Boston, New Orleans, and Chicago and had engaged in interviews at alternative schools across the Bay Area, places that educate kids who have trouble in traditional schools. We can't solve all our problems with discipline and school culture by simply hiring more teachers who come from the same communities as low-income students of color, she told me. "Students of color appreciate teachers who are from their same racial or ethnic group, but I've also spoken to girls who have had white upper-class mentor teachers who they love. They adore them because they feel they care." Students she interviewed also talked about teachers with backgrounds similar to their own who had internalized negative beliefs about those communities and told the girls that they would fail. The solution isn't the person so much as it is how they're trained, Morris said. "It's about ways to enforce—even in the credentialing process—ways for all teachers to explore their own biases." Black families deserve teachers who have thought deeply about how to build and maintain relationships with the kids they're going to teach. Sadly, we too rarely get them.

Putnam, who was a classroom teacher for five years before starting the Boggs School, says she can understand why so many of the mothers I've talked to see school as a harmful place for their children. Putnam says of herself and the other women who got the Boggs School off the ground, "We wanted to control the harm, and it felt really difficult to do that in a silo in a classroom in a school that's not rethinking what school should be."

In Atlanta, thirty-eight-year-old Zahra Alabanza helped found the Anna Julia Cooper Learning and Liberation Center. The school, which opened in September 2017, is named after the late-nineteenth- and early-twentieth-century scholar, educator, and activist who is sometimes called the mother of black feminism. It's a nontraditional school that's run by people of color, primarily black women. Alabanza's sons, who are thirteen and ten, are among the dozen students, who range in age from six to thirteen. They learn at their own pace, and the adults in leadership routinely ask what the students want to learn and how. Alabanza rejects the notion that the goal of education is to get children college ready. Instead, her priority is to show her sons all the possibilities available to them, with college being just one option.

Alabanza has a master's degree in social work and taught at DePaul University in Chicago. Traditional academia has been a central part of her own training, but she sees the value in getting her sons out into the real world, where they can learn by doing and see for themselves things they might otherwise only read about. She remembers taking her boys on a cross-country trip to the Grand Canyon. The fourteen-day absence triggered questions from their schools. "I almost had CPS called on me," she says, recalling the possibility that child protective services might intervene. "That was a defining moment for me." Faced with having her parental rights threatened because she chose to engage her sons in a learning activity outside school, Alabanza eventually chose something different. She calls pulling her children out of traditional education "the most radical thing I have ever done."

But creating an alternative is hard work. Alabanza acknowledges the difficulties of building an institution and says the Anna Julia Cooper Learning and Liberation Center is a work in progress and highly experimental. "At least our children who are there are safe," she tells me. "We can't possibly do as much harm as the public school system is doing." The challenge with new educational initiatives like these is how to keep them funded and growing. Cincinnati, where Is and I live, was from 1993 to 2010 home to an enrichment program called Sankofa. Its name refers to a West African Adinkra symbol that encourages retrieving anything valuable that's at risk of being forgotten or left behind. For nearly two decades, Sankofa convened groups of black high school students on Saturdays to talk African and African American history. It helped teenagers develop critical thinking and communication skills through conversations about current events and offered an annual black college tour. Kimya Moyo, its founder, ran the program, and her three youngest children were participants. But eventually Sankofa ran out of steam. "I didn't have any money. It was all volunteers," she tells me. Moyo, who is seventy, also struggled to keep the program relevant. The explosion in social media and digital technology shifted how young people digested information. When she thinks about how to rebirth the program, one thing is clear: "I need young people at the helm of this," she says.

I could be one of the youngish people to help Moyo revive Sankofa. I could learn from her what pitfalls to avoid, what local partners to involve, and how to keep young people and their families coming back. There's something beautiful about the prospect of helping to keep a black community institution alive. But what I have already learned in the two years since Is was born is that for the motivated parent, it's easy to get overly ambitious and stretched too thin. There are endless opportunities to get involved and improve some system that affects your family's life. When I was desperate for suitable childcare, I beat myself up for not having devoted more time and energy to lobbying for quality, subsidized childcare before I became a parent and immediately needed it. Now that my daughter is two, I toy with the idea of starting a preschool cooperative like Little Maroons, Las Semillitas, or Rice & Beans, where a lot of my Oakland-area friends have shaped their children's early education. I know that as a parent of a school-aged child, I'm in for years of feeling pulled in different directions, unsure of where to devote my limited resources.

But in addition to seeking out and building alternatives, we need to organize in the schools where most black children are educated. That belief guides Jessica Black's work. On that hot July day in her backyard, she reminds me that while innovative and culturally appropriate programs for black students are ideal, they don't have room for everyone, and they're often too expensive for low-income families. So ensuring quality education for all black children means demanding policy changes at the high-poverty schools where most are concentrated. "We have no choice but to continue to fight," she tells me. "Our babies are still going to these schools as an option."

At the Black Organizing Project (BOP), Black runs the Bettering Our School System, or BOSS, campaign. She and other organizers and lawyers train parents how to advocate for their students during suspension and expulsion hearings and IEP meetings. Often families don't know what students' rights are or how to claim those rights, and Black works to change that. She also makes sure no parent ever has to go to a meeting about her child unprepared or without support. Recently she accompanied a mother whose middle school son hadn't been receiving necessary special education services. As a team, the women succeeded in getting him placed at a new school that's better suited for students on the autism spectrum. At an expulsion hearing for a middle school girl with a diagnosed disability, Black held and entertained a toddler so the mother could focus on the case pending against her older child. Before the hearing began, she reassured the mother that the proceedings were not a reflection on her parenting. She made a statement on behalf of the family to the administrative panel hearing the case. She serves families however they need her, Black tells me. And she goes wherever black families are. The tech boom is raising housing costs and pushing many low- and middle-income longtime San Franciscans and Oaklanders farther east and into Pittsburg, Antioch, and Contra Costa County. The BOP offices might be located in West and East Oakland, but Black goes wherever black communities are growing as a result of displacement.

The work takes her all over California. She's part of an effort led by black students and parents to get police out of all schools in the state by 2020. Black and fellow organizers for justice in education have already had some victories at the local level. In 2015, Oakland Unified's school board voted to invest at least $2.3 million to expand restorative justice practices in its schools. That same year the district eliminated willful defiance as grounds for suspension at any grade level.[18]

I expect Black to get excited about these victories, but she doesn't. Instead, she says while these policy changes are important, they're not enough. "There has to be a real shift in the culture and climate," Black tells me. "Great, we won willful defiance. Implementation is different. While it looks like a win on paper, we're still finding kids that are getting kicked out and they're [school staffers] just recategorizing how they're doing it." The ideology that maintains huge, race-based differences in how children are educated and disciplined has to be dismantled, Black says.

We sit quietly for a moment before I ask, "But isn't the ideology white supremacy?"

She nods. "You've got to dismantle it completely."

CHAPTER 7

Body

WHEN MY DAUGHTER IS AROUND EIGHTEEN MONTHS OLD, I BUY US A children's board book called *C Is for Consent* after I see it mentioned on a feminist listserv. I want to start teaching her that she has the right to say no to any touch she doesn't want, at any time and without explanation. This seems a good way to start the conversation.

There's something awkward about the book's earnest efforts to communicate how inclusive it intends to be. The opening scene situates the young protagonist, Finn, at a small family gathering that's attended by two interracial couples, a person in a wheelchair, and a same-sex couple that's never seen or heard from again. But fine, I see where the writer, Eleanor Morrison, and illustrator, Faye Orlove, are going. This book is for *us*, it screams, the conscious and the woke. In one scene Grandma goes in for a hug, but Finn hesitates. His dad tells him, "That's okay. You don't have to give anyone a hug if you don't feel like it!"[1] In another scene, an aunt and uncle beckon Finn over, fighting over whose lap he should sit on. Finn passes, explaining that his parents say he doesn't have to sit on laps if he doesn't want to.

There's no rhyming or fanciful pictures, so *C Is for Consent* doesn't hold my daughter's attention. We read it a few times; then she starts to toss it aside. Still, I keep it out in our home and sometimes pack it in the bag that follows her on outings to relatives' houses. I want all of the adults who care for her to flip through it and think about how even actions we intend as affectionate and harmless can shape how kids think about their own instincts and bodies. I like that the book offers alternatives to close touch—high fives and fist bumps instead of hugs and kisses. I like that it points out that it's weird to give a child a gift and then ask for a hug or a kiss in return. By explicitly addressing things that have been normalized over the course of my life, the book—however awkward in its presentation—gets me thinking about all the ways we're taught to override our annoyance, disgust, exhaustion, or lack of interest and just do what the person with more power wants us to do.

But I don't have this conversation outright with family members. I never say, "Please don't press Is to give you a kiss or hug if she first says no." I just slide the book into strategic places and intervene as subtly as possible (usually through distraction) when I see an uncomfortable situation unfolding. Once again, I'm reminded of the courage that good parenting demands. If I can't be direct with adult family members about supporting my daughter's bodily autonomy, how will I be direct in letting her know she should claim it for herself? If I am afraid to offend or alienate now, will I be afraid to offend or alienate when it's time to talk with Is about sexual violence, safer sex, and telling a lover or a doctor what she wants for her body?

When I was in my late teens or early twenties, I asked my own mother why we'd never had The Talk™ that other kids and teenagers seemed to have with their parents about sex. She said something along the lines of, "You were smart. I knew you'd figure it out." I remember thinking that had been both a cop-out and a huge risk on her part. I may have been book smart, but I didn't know how to fill in the significant gaps left by my school's sex ed curriculum, which I remember as a blur of close-up photos of genitals disfigured by sexually transmitted infections. I was frustrated that she'd let her own discomfort trump initiating a conversation that could've better prepared me for life as a sexual being. But now that I have a child, I kind of get it. Life is always moving so quickly, and sometimes it's easier to just keep putting off the difficult talks until you've convinced yourself they're not necessary anyway.

I want to forge a different path with my daughter. I want to talk with her about her body and about sex, and I want to feel confident doing it. If a decade from now is anything like today, she's not likely to get what she needs at school. Fewer than 40 percent of US high schools and just 14 percent of middle schools provide all of the nineteen topics identified by the Centers for Disease Control and Prevention as critical sexual health information. The list includes learning how to correctly put on a condom and how to identify healthy and respectful relationships. Only about half of teenagers receive school instruction about birth control before they have sex for the first time, according to the National Institutes of Health. This matters. Young people who receive formal sex ed are more likely to delay their first sexual encounter and use birth control when they do decide to have sex. Geography plays a big part in what young people learn. Only twenty states require that sex ed in schools be medically accurate, and eighteen states require that students learn that sex should only happen within marriage. Ohio is one of them. The state's Abstinence Education Law requires that sex ed programs "teach that conceiving children out of wedlock is likely to have harmful consequences for the child, the child's parents, and society." There's no requirement that sex ed curricula in our state mention the terms "healthy relationships," "sexual assault," or "consent."[2]

When abstinence, misinformation, and scare tactics are at the foundation of schools' sex ed curricula, of course young people turn to other sources. Online porn tops the list. In 2016, Emily Rothman, an associate professor at Boston University's School of Public Health, conducted a study in which she asked seventy-two primarily black and Latino high schoolers ages sixteen and seventeen their primary source of information about sex. Most reported that it was porn. Parents tend to be incredibly naive about all this. In February 2018, the *New York Times Magazine* ran a story called "What Teenagers Are Learning from Online Porn" and reported preliminary analysis of data obtained from a 2016 Indiana University survey of more than six hundred pairs of children and their parents: "Half as many parents thought their 14- and 18-year-olds had seen porn as had in fact watched it. And depending on the sex act, parents underestimated what their kids saw by as much as 10 times." Of course, they're seeing the same things many of us see when we go online for porn: facials, gang bangs, rough oral sex, and a whole category that classifies black bodies as "ebony." Phones make it easier than ever to access explicit material, and it often happens in the early teen years. Boys typically first see porn around the age of thirteen and girls around fourteen, according to the *Times* report.[3]

Young people want to talk to their parents and other people they trust about sex more than we think. In 2013, the Illinois Caucus for Adolescent Health (ICAH) published a report called "Given and Chosen: Talking to Family About Sexuality."[4] The progressive sexual health organization interviewed and surveyed 470 young people between the ages of sixteen and twenty-two in Chicago and nationally. Participating youth reported that they didn't feel encouraged by family to talk about sex and that this lack of openness was the biggest barrier they faced to making healthy decisions about sex. They craved emotional support through conversation and recognized that this was where the internet fell short. But too often family members were dismissive or judgmental, or else they had inaccurate information, which shut down conversations, the young people reported. "It's really about making a climate where you can ask anything," says Yamani Hernandez, a mother of two who was executive director of ICAH at the time of the study. "That extends beyond sex." Hernandez recommends being ready to talk about even the most delicate topics and not letting our body language shut down a conversation before it starts.

Relaxing could go a long way toward feeling prepared. I think parents are often afraid that our children will expect us to be experts, that they'll ask us something we don't know how to answer and then lose faith when we admit we don't have fully formed ideas on a topic. But maybe we should trust that the conversation will be just that, a back-and-forth with opinions and information moving in both directions. Cat Brooks, the Oakland-based community organizer who has a twelve-year-old, has found that her daughter is way ahead of her when it comes to thinking about gender identity. It makes sense, Brooks says. Her daughter is growing up in a different time and place, and a childhood in the boundary-pushing Bay Area is going to yield different results. "For her that's second nature. It's nothing that she had to learn or unlearn," Brooks tells me. "I'm cooking dinner, and she's sitting at the counter, and we're talking, and she said, 'I don't think so-and-so is gay, I think he's pansexual.' And I was like, 'What the fuck is that?' Sort of dropped the frying pan." Brooks recounts the story laughing, and it's the kind of conversation I want to have with my daughter someday—impromptu, relaxed, and with plenty of room for humor and learning.

When I think about future talks with my daughter, I feel most unsure how to prepare her for the possibility of violence, especially at the hands of people she has come to know and trust. I'm not sure how to teach her how to be vigilant but open, trusting but not naive. She is a toddler, and at this point in her development I have tried to create a protected space in our home and in the small orbit in which she moves, an oasis where she as a black girl can feel free and empowered and dignified. That's meant the right books and the decision not to spank and all the organic, whole foods and on and on. But when the wave of #MeToo accusations and revelations hits late in 2017, I'm reminded that I don't have nearly as much control as I think I do.

I have to guard against my own paranoia. When I change her diaper after she's been in the care of someone new, I look closely to make sure her labia and anus aren't swollen, discolored, or irritated. When, at nearly eighteen months, she takes to smiling during clothes changes, pointing to her nipple and calling it "nana," the word she also uses for food, I try not to imagine all kinds of dark possibilities. I ask her, "Who calls it that?" and drop it when she doesn't say anything I recognize. (As I write this, just after she's turned two, I see this habit in a different light. Now that she has more words, she sometimes points to her nipple and smiles and says, "Ihbel have milk, milk," a kind of joke about how while Mom may have milk in there, she doesn't, and wouldn't that be hilarious if she did? It's a reminder that I can't divine our way to safety.) As she gets older and her language and ability to reason get better, I can check in with her about touching and safety. Eventually, I'll be able to establish norms with her, coach her on what to do if any number of things happen. But, again, there will be limits to what we can control. And how do I teach her to feel free, curious, and confident in a world that will sometimes be vile and disrespectful to her not only because of her race but also because of her sex?

One day in November 2017, I'm online catching up on the latest #MeToo accusations. More dominos are falling: Charlie

Rose. John Conyers. Jeffrey Tambor. I've missed a tweet from earlier in the month that went viral. Writer Jennifer Wright had tweeted, "Hey women, retweet if you've ever been shown a penis you did not want or expect to see."[5] I'm floored by the number of interactions with the tweets—retweets, likes, responses. I think of the most memorable time I'd been caught off guard by a random penis. When I was in grad school, I often had a late-night subway commute from Columbia's campus home to Brooklyn. This particular night, I glanced up from a copy of *Hiroshima* to find a naked penis inches from my face. Its owner had used his briefcase to shield the forced viewing from the other people in the subway car. I was the sole observer of his spectacle, trapped. Managing to shake off the shock and disgust, I stood up. I yelled at him, putting into words what he had done, thinking someone on the train might take an interest and come to my aid. No one did. I kicked him in his back as he scurried off to another car. Wright's tweet puts me right back in those moments. I hadn't talked about it much since. I text two friends, "Can you imagine woman after woman just flashing her vag and men not even thinking to mention it because it's so commonplace in their lives?" The answer, of course, is no. The issue here is power, not anatomy, and taken as a whole, women simply don't wield as much power as men do in public spaces, in the workplace, or anywhere.

My daughter will have to live through this, the electric jolt of having something thrust upon her that she didn't ask for and doesn't want. Men will broadcast on the street what they want to do to her body. A boss or a pastor or a mentor will nonchalantly touch her in a way that makes her feel gross, and she'll wonder if she's crazy for feeling gross. I know these things will happen. I just pray none of it happens while she's still a child. It makes me sick that this is the best I can hope for her.

I am driving one day during those same weeks of rapid-fire #MeToo accusations when I catch bell hooks being interviewed on the radio by the *New Yorker*'s David Remnick.[6] The problem, hooks says, is that "we raise males to believe that violence is how you get what you want and that you have a right to violence." She is talking about emotional intelligence and encouraging therapy. Unlike so much of the commentary I've heard on #MeToo, hooks is going straight to answering the questions that have consumed me: What's with the deep compulsion to flash and shame and overpower and trap us? Where does it come from? What is this ability to compart-mentalize behavior into that which is decent and respectful and worthy of human interaction and that which is brutish and deranged? Where others dance around these root ques-tions, hooks puts it plainly. The problem is patriarchy. She is seemingly unbothered by whether her word choice is too academic, too off-putting, whether it will make some listen-ers tune out. In naming the problem and in using this word especially, hooks rejects the notion that the problem is individ-ual bad actors. Instead, she says, the problem is a system that teaches us all that expressing violence and rage and entitlement is a legitimate way for boys and men to get what they want.

By calling out the system and the fact that we're all impli-cated, by refusing to hedge in anticipation of the "not all men" chorus, hooks is connecting this #MeToo moment to Daniel Holtzclaw, the Oklahoma City cop convicted of rape and sexual assault after coercing eight black women into sex acts. She's connecting #MeToo to the men who commit mass shootings and turn out to have a history of domestic violence, from the Texas church shooter to the Las Vegas shooter to the man who shot two New York City police officers in December 2014 after first shooting an ex-girlfriend in the stomach. She's connecting it to Brock Turner, who was convicted of sexually assaulting an unconscious girl behind a dumpster on Stanford's campus. She's connecting it to Elliot Rodger, who shot up UC Santa Barbara students because all the pretty white girls he felt he deserved weren't interested in him.

Hooks's solution puts people raising kids on the hook. "We've got to be willing to challenge the way we parent," she tells Remnick. "This has to begin on the level of family." I read the 2004 book in which she's expounded on these ideas, *The Will to Change: Men, Masculinity and Love*, cheering and underlining as I read. I also send a copy to Is's dad. I want him to help me teach our daughter that the current, widely held understanding of masculinity is not natural or correct or anything she has to accept or embrace. All around me, friends with young children are thinking about how to be intentional and consistent about teaching something different.

Vashti Rutledge is a former program officer in women's health who now runs the Cincinnati branch of the Family Independence Initiative, an organization that works to combat poverty. We also grew up together, and she has a daughter who's just a few months younger than Is. Rutledge tells me that what's stood out in the recent flood of celebrity #MeToo stories was the account of the woman who accused NBC's Matt Lauer of assaulting her in his office. After the assault, she passed out and had to be taken to a nurse. The woman said she felt ashamed and afraid of losing her job and so didn't report Lauer at the time. Rutledge wonders about that NBC employee: What has taught you that you don't have a right to say no? She and I talk about this in the context of how to keep our girl babies safe, and she looks at me with genuine fear and confusion in her eyes.

I feel as incredulous around some of this stuff as my friend. I can't imagine a job I want so badly that I keep my mouth shut after someone's thrown a lock on their office door, bent me over a chair, and raped me. I have to check my immediate, internal response to many of these accounts, the belief that black women typically don't put up with as much shit from men. I read Lupita Nyong'o's account in the *Times* about repeatedly and successfully beating back Harvey Weinstein's advances and feel validated. We just don't bow to abusive male power as easily, I tell myself. We see it for what it is—empty, a cover for insecurity, the product of overblown egos that can usually be deflated with a direct and forceful no. I hear Jenifer Lewis, the self-proclaimed Mother of Black Hollywood, on the podcast *Another Round* talk about her career in theater. "I just don't think there was a casting couch, not for us African Americans," she tells the hosts. "My first review in New York City, the headline was, 'Hurricane Lewis hits New York.' Now who gonna pull out their little bitty penis in front of a hurricane?" Again, I feel affirmed.[7]

But deep down I know that this is a defense mechanism and that I'm blaming victims, assuming that I can imagine what they've been through. I don't like it when black folk in my family or Facebook feed defend Bill Cosby against his (mostly white) accusers, going on and on about how these accusers knew what they were getting into and how their own skills of discernment are superior. I remind myself that it was a black woman, Anita Hill, who made sexual harassment in the workplace a national issue and who explained to a congressional committee of white men why women often don't confront or report their more powerful harassers at the time. Surely this brilliant woman would've gotten herself out of the mess that was Clarence Thomas if her blackness had given her some kind of superpower. The "we're smarter than that" narrative is just another version of the "you're smart enough to figure it out" message about sexuality that I got as a kid. In both, individual girls and women bear all the responsibility and take all the blame when things go wrong. I don't want to pass these messages on to my daughter.

Shaping young people's thinking about power and healthy relationships is, like most sex ed, largely left up to families. In 2015, California became the first state to mandate consent education in all public schools, and to date only eight states and the District of Columbia require that consent be mentioned.[8] I want to know what black boys are learning at home in the #MeToo age. Zahra Alabanza tells me consent has always been part of the dialogue she has with her sons, who are ten and thirteen. She'll watch them approach someone for an embrace and at times interrupt with "Did you ask if you could give them a hug?" Alabanza wants her boys to be conscious in what too often become rote, unconscious interactions. "They are male-bodied people, and they will have a sense of power that we don't in this world," she tells me.

When we speak, Alabanza has recently found her older son with a detailed drawing of a woman giving a man oral sex. She confronted him about it and learned that he had drawn the image after seeing it acted out in porn. She asked him a series of questions, including "How do you know it feels good for her?" Her son admitted that he didn't. This opened a conversation about pleasure and consent. "It's really more fun if everybody is being pleased," she told him. If not, "it's not going to be good for you, and you should stop." Then Alabanza went a step further. She told her son to put a banana in his mouth. When he took it out, she asked him to think about the sex act he'd seen onscreen alongside the sensation he'd just felt. "He gave me this look of, 'Wow, I didn't think about these things,'" she tells me.

Her story reminds me of an interview I listened to in the spring of 2017. Richard Rohr, a Franciscan spiritual teacher who works with men, told the interviewer that earlier in his career he'd done a cross-cultural study of male initiation rites. What he learned from looking around the world was that "unless the male was led on journeys of powerlessness, he would always abuse power . . . The male just can't handle power unless he's somehow touched upon vulnerability, powerlessness."[9] Alabanza is leading these journeys of powerlessness in her own home for her sons' sake and for the world's.

It's also true that this country gives black boys and men, like Latino and Native boys and men, plenty of opportunities to experience powerlessness and vulnerability. From police departments' stop-and-frisk policies to the loss of bodily autonomy experienced in the jails and prisons where they're overrepresented, the carceral state hangs the threat of violation over some boys' and men's heads, too. As Yamani Hernandez sees it, the question is, how do we acknowledge the various experiences of boys and men as they relate to issues of sexuality and consent? Hernandez, formerly of ICAH, is now the executive director of the National Network of Abortion Funds and a longtime reproductive justice advocate. As the mother of two sons, ages twelve and seventeen, she can see clearly how the women-led movement she's a part of overlooks the nuances of boys' lives. "The [reproductive justice] movement script about men or boys is just about police brutality and making sure they don't get killed," she tells me. "We [as women] want to be seen in our entire totality and complexity from birth, and we reduce the issues that we care about to whether a black boy gets to grow up."

Hernandez mentions how common it is for young black men with celebrity status to say that a childhood babysitter was an early sexual experience, as the rapper Drake did in a song, or to brag about becoming sexually active as a child, as has rapper Lil' Wayne. "No, that's rape," she says. "We perpetuate this stereotype about the barbarism of men and boys and are unwilling to see the vulnerability of boys and men." When they've talked about sex, Hernandez's seventeen-year-old son has asked where his own rights come into play. "It's a hard conversation because you sound ridiculous if you say, 'Men's rights are bullshit,'" she says. "How do you tell your male child that?"

Men's rights activists (or MRAs), whose hatred of feminism fuels their belief that society actually oppresses and marginalizes men and not women, have undermined the possibility that we can have a balanced, nuanced conversation about men's rights. The challenge is to not let MRAs control the narrative around harm done to men and to figure out new ways to offer the boys in our lives the consideration they deserve.

Hernandez got one of her first lessons around consent and the male body soon after her older son's birth. She was twenty-two at the time and hadn't given much thought to whether he'd be circumcised. When hospital staff told her he'd be taken for the procedure, she didn't think twice. "We went home, and I was looking at his penis, and it was bloody and wounded," she tells me. "I was like, 'Oh my God, what did I do?'" Five years later when she had her second son, she had done research and decided that he would not be circumcised. "That was my first act of saying, 'This is his body, and he gets to decide what happens to it,'" she says. Recently she was with the older boy at a doctor's appointment when the health-care provider strongly suggested to her that he get the HPV vaccine, which is recommended for children as young as eleven. Hernandez stood strong: "It's his decision."

ॐ

THE NUMBERS TELL US HOW CRITICAL IT IS THAT BLACK teenagers have the information and support they need to make decisions about how to keep their bodies safe and healthy. Cases of chlamydia, gonorrhea, and syphilis are on the rise and have been since 2014. That means more high school– and college-aged young people getting sick. Youth between the ages of fifteen and twenty-four make up a quarter of the sexually active US population but account for half of all sexually transmitted infections (STIs) acquired each year. Black communities are especially hard-hit. The chlamydia rate for young black men aged fifteen to nineteen is 8.8 times that of their white counterparts. For black girls in that age group, it's 4.5 times higher. Black youth between the ages of thirteen and twenty-four account for 57 percent of all new HIV infections. In 2015 I interviewed Dr. Melissa Gilliam, a Chicago-based expert in pediatric and adolescent gynecology, for a story I was writing on youth and birth control. She reminded me that some of the most talked-about methods of contraception—IUDs, the pill, hormonal implants—are not barriers and don't protect against the transmission of STIs. So while the public often hears that the teen birth rate has continually declined over the past twenty years, those celebratory headlines don't tell the whole story. "One of the greatest causes of infertility is STIs," she says. "That's where the public-health alarm needs to be."[10]

For that same story, I spoke with Dr. Stephanie Teal, a clinician and researcher in Colorado who has worked extensively with young women of color on accessing birth control. She told me that while IUDs and implants (often called long-acting reversible contraceptives, or LARCs) have been instrumental in bringing down that teen birth rate, research that she had conducted but not yet published showed that young women are slightly less likely to use a condom with LARCs than they are if they're on a short-acting birth control

method like the pill.[11] As I see it, while young people are having fewer unwanted pregnancies, they haven't internalized key
messages about how to stay healthy and alive.

I feel out of touch and a little worried when I watch an
episode of *Atlanta*, the award-winning existential black dram-
edy series. In the episode, the character Van chats with her
friends, black women who appear to be in their midtwenties,
about birth control. The IUD is mentioned and its merits
debated. Nadine, the one friend who says she uses condoms
(or any kind of barrier method), is ridiculed. "Bitch, how
old are you?" Van asks, and the others pile on. Nadine claps
back: "You know what? I don't have kids, and I also don't have
HPV, trick."[12]

We need as many Nadines as possible spreading truths
about sexual health. Popular culture may be a last line of
defense. The Trump administration is committed to promot-
ing abstinence-only programs and has cut hundreds of millions
of dollars from community-based sex education programs for
teens and their parents. Nearly four thousand health centers
across the nation that receive federal grants to provide STI
testing and treatment, birth control, and cancer screenings to
low-income young people are at risk of losing funding because
of the administration's refusal to support a comprehensive
approach to reproductive health. The United States has long
lagged behind European countries in allowing prudishness and
religious fundamentalism to override public health concerns,
but these days we're backsliding even further. Under Trump,
officials at the CDC were banned in 2017 from using certain
words or phrases in budget documents. When the nation's

top public health agency can't even use the words "diversity," "transgender," "fetus," "evidence-based," or "science-based" to prepare its budget, young people are forced to seek out online resources, such as Scarleteen and Bedsider, for accurate, inclusive information about their bodies and sex lives.[13]

Ignorance is already too often the norm when it comes to sexual health. Throughout her years as a youth educator on these issues, Yamani Hernandez has heard all of the misinformation young people sometimes circulate. At a girls' program years ago, she heard that since you can't get pregnant from anal sex, condoms weren't necessary when engaging in the act. The girls often centered the concept of virginity and talked about what one could do and still claim that she's a virgin. (Having anal sex wasn't *really* sex, she was told.) Hernandez remembers that basic anatomy was a major blind spot among some youth she's encountered. "Most kids do not know what a clitoris is. They don't know the urethra. They're just like—'hole.'"

If you have a clitoris but don't know that it exists or what it's for, you can't tell a sexual partner to focus there. You can't redirect a partner who's pounding away at your vagina without much foreplay, convinced by porn that this is what women want. In short, you can't center your own pleasure. I want my daughter to understand what makes her feel good and to know that she deserves pleasure. I hope she delays sex until she's ready for it emotionally. Once she starts, I don't want her suffering through bad encounters with selfish, clueless partners.

When I ask parents whether they address sexual pleasure with their kids, they typically mention how they've handled masturbation when it's come up with toddlers and preschool-aged children. These conversations tend to be basic, they say, more focused on privacy and where to do it (in a bedroom, not at the dinner table) than anything else. I have no plans to dissuade her from touching herself and wonder how else I can give my two-year-old the message that she should trust and feel ownership of her body. I remember something I learned at Detroit's Allied Media Conference in the summer of 2017. Along with Is and my mom, I attended a workshop called Mamas and Grandmas for the Revolution, at which participants traded strategies for raising the next generation of radical thinkers and doers. Hong Gwi-Seok, a Korean American elder, grandmother, and poet was one of the session's facilitators. She had also been my beloved Iyengar yoga teacher more than a decade earlier when I lived in Milwaukee, so I was especially interested in her advice on how to get children to feel confident and strong in their bodies. That day, Hong emphasized the importance of introducing choice early on. She said leaving healthy food options around the house and breastfeeding on demand are two ways to teach even the youngest child that she can know and satiate her own hunger. This begins a habit of listening to her body, identifying a desire, and moving toward it.

By the time they're teenagers, it's hard to know whether young people are acting on what they actually desire sexually or what they think they should desire. According to that *New York Times* report on youth and porn, a lot of teens— especially boys—believe what they see in porn is "realistic" and that the pleasure performed there is actual pleasure. This is why Alabanza's banana-in-the-mouth demonstration is so powerful. She made her thirteen-year-old son embody and consider a potential partner's experience. At the time, she also asked whether the porn he watched had featured anyone who was black or a person of color, another check to see whether he was unwittingly allowing his budding sexual identity to be colonized by someone else's ideas around beauty, pleasure, and power.

I asked Alabanza what she did with what she learned from her son during this conversation. After all, he'd been forthcoming about how watching porn had made him feel. He'd been open to considering new perspectives. What did he get in exchange for his honesty? For one thing, she said, he got her thinking about how to give him an age- and culturally appropriate experience that acknowledges his drive to develop a sexual self. This could mean magazines, she told me, or those progressive sex ed books from the 1970s with realistic images. She said she'd also started talking with a local feminist bookstore about organizing two groups—one for youth peer-to-peer sex ed, the other for parents grappling with how to talk about sex with their kids. The thirteen-year-old also got a piece of advice from his mother: "If you're into girls, get you a lesbian homegirl and learn from her," she told him, "not your homeboys."

Because I didn't have this kind of openness around sex when I was growing up, I need clear, practical tips for how to establish a home environment that's sex positive. I get some tools from LisaGay Hamilton, the actor who lives in Los Angeles with her husband and their two sons, ages fifteen and seven. In an effort to get the boys into the habit of talking at the dinner table, Hamilton and her husband put questions inside a hat to prompt mealtime conversation. Some topics that have come up: What does it mean to be safe with drugs? Is the pull-out method a reliable form of contraception? This last question created an opportunity for a necessary intervention. Hamilton's older son strenuously argued that yes, pulling out is good contraception until he finally, when pressed, admitted that he didn't actually know what the word "contraception" meant.

Meeting moments like this with humor and real talk rather than shame or judgment creates a safe space where young people know they can be vulnerable. Hamilton tells me the conversations extend beyond the dinner table. Her fifteen-year-old has shared with her his frustration over erections that last too long and the perils of itchy pubic hair. "Apparently these days boys wanna shave and pluck it. Who knew?" she says. "I am in awe of [his] willingness to share about his body with us."

Being a brave and comfortable communicator on the topic of sex and the body is critical when it comes to setting the stage for safe, pleasurable sex. It's also a must in the doctor's office. I'm reminded of this when I report that magazine article on birth control and learn that often doctors' and nurses' perceptions of a patient's reproductive needs can override what that patient may actually want for herself. One concern about LARCs—those long-acting reversible contraceptives that guard against pregnancy for years at a time—is that they're provider controlled, meaning they need to be placed in the uterus (IUD) or arm (implant) by a health practitioner.

Someone who has a LARC can't simply wake up one morning, decide to stop using it, and take it out herself that day. She needs to schedule an appointment to have the birth control removed.

These forms of contraception are sometimes called "set it and forget it" methods, and some reproductive justice activists have encouraged that we take a closer look at how race, class, and power play into these patient-provider interactions. After all, as scholar and *Killing the Black Body* author Dorothy Roberts told me when I interviewed her for the story, "The idea that we've gone past eugenicist thinking, past racist thinking, past population-control ideology, is just false." Some research supports the claim. I read a study that showed that low-income black and Latina women felt more pressure to limit their family size in conversations with providers than did middle-class white women. In another, providers were more likely to recommend the IUD to low-income black and Latina patients than to low-income white patients with comparable reproductive health histories.[14]

One way to protect against provider bias and center the patient's preferences, I learn while reporting, is to standardize how providers counsel patients on birth control. Anu Manchikanti Gomez and Liza Fuentes, two public health researchers, suggest what's called "a woman-centered framework," which prioritizes the patient's stated reproductive and health goals and preferences over what's most effective in preventing pregnancy. This approach sounds great, but it doesn't mean much if we don't raise young people to know and confidently express what they want.

Just as I had to when I was pregnant, I want my daughter to be comfortable talking about her body to people in white coats who toss around jargon and speak quickly and with authority. I want her to be able to take a deep breath, center, and express what she actually wants for herself, regardless of whatever assumptions someone is making about her, her sex life, or what her fertility might mean for the county's WIC or welfare rolls. I want her to feel OK saying, "I don't want hormonal birth control," if she is like her mother and doesn't like the way it makes her feel. I want her to be able to look a doubtful or pushy health-care provider in the eye and resist any efforts to tell her she can't be responsible with the birth control pill or she won't be able to negotiate condom use with a partner every time. If she knows she doesn't want to get a period or she wants a hysterectomy at an age considered by some to be too young, I want her to be able to advocate for herself in the examining room.

These interactions with medical staff may be far off, as are interactions with possible lovers or harassers. It's my job to prepare her for these conversations, and teaching her to know and trust her body starts now.

CHAPTER 8

Spirit

WHEN I WAS SEVEN MONTHS PREGNANT WITH IS, I WENT ON A WEEK-long silent meditation retreat in western Massachusetts. It was my first time at this particular center but not my first time committing to sit and walk and eat in silence and to spend my days and evenings receiving Buddhist teachings, or the dharma, in an austere, spacious hall filled with other spiritual seekers. This retreat, like others I had been to in California, was specifically for people of color, or else reserved a sizable portion of spots for those who self-identified as such. This acknowledgment of race, of ethnicity, of culture was what had drawn me into East Bay Meditation Center (EBMC), the Oakland practice space where I began sitting and attending dharma talks in 2009, soon after moving to the San Francisco Bay Area. I had first been introduced to Buddhism and meditation at a Cincinnati center five years earlier, but it wasn't until I found EBMC, with its many black and Asian teachers and its dharma talks that touched on issues of power and social justice, that I began to see how I might find a home in Buddhism.

When I think of this retreat, I remember the shapeless red maternity dress I wore a lot in that third trimester. I think of how ravenous I was when I arrived late at the center that July night. (My travel had been delayed.) I remember how good it felt to be welcomed by a black man at the front desk who, after checking me in, ushered me to a long table filled with soup and bread and hardboiled eggs and other nourishing foods for my tired, big body. I had been on the road a lot that spring and summer—to Seattle, Memphis, Pittsburgh, and New York for work. I knew this would be my last bit of travel before I settled in at home to await the baby's arrival. Here, in the form of this retreat, was a perfect way to soften my focus on the world around me and turn inward to focus on how to give this forming being inside me as calm and safe an arrival as possible.

Even before Is was born I thought about how to nurture in her a spiritual life. I want to help her find an inner compass so that she knows how to manage her emotions, love herself always, and turn inward for answers rather than always looking to someone or something else. For some of us, modeling spiritual development looks like simply taking our children along to church or mosque or whatever faith community we belong to. For Is and me, that's been a challenge, because I've moved away from the place my community was located. More importantly, because of their focus on silence and stillness, Buddhist *sanghas* ("communities" in Pali, one of the languages of the Buddhist texts) aren't typically set up for families with young children. I can't picture my squirmy, loud toddler in any of the meditation spaces I've been in. We would be disruptive, and what would such a solemn environment have to offer a little one? Still, I see contemplative practice and faith community as necessary foundations for human development and principled political action, so I'm determined to answer this question: where does my family fit in?

I don't identify as Christian. I'm a black American from semirural Ohio, and culturally, yes, I'm Christian. But that doesn't accurately describe my spiritual orientation. I believe that Buddhism offers the clearest, most compelling teachings on the nature of the mind and that Christianity—as analyzed by the likes of Howard Thurman and Thomas Merton— offers the clearest, most compelling teachings on love. I have learned things from the Old and New Testaments, but I'm not called to deepen my study of those texts. Growing up, we went to church as a family occasionally, but my introduction to the black church came primarily through the expectation that I would do what the other kids in my neighborhood did and what my mom and her peers had done before us.

We went to Sunday school and usually stayed afterward for church service. We sang in the choir. We were part of the Christmas pageant. During the summer, we went to a weeklong vacation Bible school. The little white and brick church was right down the street from my house, not even a five-minute walk. It was also, in some ways, a center of our social lives as kids. Sunday school was fun. Mrs. Warner was sweet and firm and helped us make art projects out of popsicle sticks and construction paper. The choir was fun.

Mrs. Ramseur (who also watched me in those hours between when school ended and when my mom got home from work and whose granddaughter Sarah was my closest friend) played piano beautifully and taught us to be confident and strong in our voices. It was fun to watch the woman from down the street catch the spirit and fall out or to watch as people talked in tongues and rhythmically raised themselves high up on their tiptoes. When people got baptized, usually in their preteen years, it felt important to witness them dunked into the shallow pool hidden under the pulpit and to watch them emerge somehow new, more mature, publicly committed to Christ.

I didn't get baptized. I hadn't even been christened. I happily immersed myself in the activities (most of which involved, at some point, good food and sugary drinks) but held some of the more involved content at arm's length and with a kind of respectful detachment. I was scared by talk of end times and rejected any idea that those who hadn't been baptized would burn in hell while those who had were fated for heaven. In the neighborhood, some cousins' and close friends' fathers were themselves pastors or deacons, and I could see how deeply they believed these things, how what we learned in church was being reinforced for them elsewhere. Not so for me. My own maternal great-grandmother had been a preacher. A small wooden cross with an affixed drooping Jesus hung in our hallway. But other than learning a simple bedtime prayer and bowing my head for prayer during meals at family gatherings, ours wasn't a particularly Christian household.

That prayer, which my mom taught me when I was old enough to speak, went like this:

Now I lay me down to sleep
I pray the Lord my soul to keep
If I should die before I wake
I pray the Lord my soul to take

It's macabre, really, a nightly ritual devoted to the possibility that one won't wake up. But my mother taught me other, more important things about how to relate to myself and what it might mean to have a soul. Her own lack of interest in church, alongside her clearly solid moral footing, taught me that I didn't need any kind of intermediary or institution to be "good" or to have a relationship with a higher power. When I was young, that higher power was called God, but my mother never gave me the sense that I needed to have a rigid understanding around what that meant. Because of this lack of rigidity and the absence of any need to give God a particular body or shape or home, it was easy for this force to become "the universe" or "all beings" or "nature" as I became older. Later, I would think to myself that if we were a different kind of family, what I was taught might have been called ethical humanism or agnosticism, or maybe we would have gone to a Unitarian church. But we weren't that kind of family. We were black Ohioans who belonged to a particular cultural tradition, and a piece of that culture was expressed through religion. And I'm thankful that while I don't plan to pass Christian teachings on to Is, our family is passing along some of the Christian songs and prayers and practices that are woven into the black American experience. At two she can sing the opening lines of "Wade in the Water." When I put her meal in front of her and say, "I'm so thankful we have good, healthy food to eat together," she says simply, "Amen." I want to find a service we can go to that has a great choir. She needs to know when to throw a double clap into a church song.

In addition to the rituals that connect us with other people, religion can also help us learn what it means to feel centered and at peace. Church gave me some of this, but I didn't receive much instruction in how to identify, manage, and express my emotions growing up. Other than being reprimanded for expressing anger and learning that sadness is to be suppressed ("Don't cry") and makes others uncomfortable, I think many of us enter adulthood without a real handle on how to know how we feel or what to do about it. This disconnection can undermine our power, leaving us unable to access the righteous anger that can fuel change or unable to grieve when, to move on, we must reckon with loss.

I am fascinated by Is's emotional outbursts and by the force with which she expresses her opinions and preferences. Her looks can be withering, and she has perfect timing and a temper I admire. Sometimes we'll be at the playground or some other place where people are trying to engage her, and I'll coach her on how a pleasant interaction with a stranger is supposed to go. A three- or four-year-old will run up to her near the slide, and they'll stare at each other. I read in the older kid an interest and in Is a skepticism. I say something like, "You say 'Hi. I'm Isobel. What's your name?'" To which she typically responds loudly and insistently, "Ih-bel no say hi!" The look on her face communicates pure shock and genuine hurt that someone from outside her circle of intimates might approach her. I marvel at the way she rebukes the efforts of a middle-aged woman as we wait in line for the bathroom during a layover at O'Hare. "Well, aren't you just the cutest?" the woman says and is met with a blank stare. "And your little jacket!" More blank stare and a rapid head shake. "You're just being silly, girl," the woman says, turning away. I'm an introvert myself and generally avoid small talk with strangers. Still, I've learned that the occasional random, brief chat costs me nothing and can be pleasant. I want my child to be friendly, but I also appreciate that she is so innately clear on her boundaries and hasn't yet internalized the need to placate or accommodate others. She doesn't pretend to be feeling anything other than what she is.

At some point, of course, she'll have to. A few months after her first birthday, we get a book that I hope will eventually aid our conversations about how to skillfully do just that. It's a book called *Master Maasai and His Power to Choose*, and it's written by a friend named Sedara Burson. Burson is a therapist and manages a mental health clinic in Atlanta, where she lives with her four-year-old son, Maasai. In 2017, she self-published the book, which tells the story of a young boy and a set of cartoon characters who embody the different emotions living inside him, including anger, silliness, happiness, and calm. Maasai goes to school and refuses to do what his new teacher tells him. His anger has taken over, thus eclipsing the other emotions and directing his actions. Another day at school, silliness gains control and causes him to tease and distract his classmates. With the help of his parents, Maasai learns to choose which emotion controls his behavior at any given time. Unlike the similarly themed Pixar movie *Inside Out*, Burson's protagonist is a black boy, and his supportive parents and teacher are black as well.

Burson is a Cincinnati native and gave a reading of the book at a branch of our local public library in November 2017. Is and I went and were among a group of about two dozen people, half adults and half kids, all black. This felt significant—an intergenerational room of black people thinking together about our mental health and how to control our responses to whatever the world throws at us.

I have done stints in therapy and found some of them helpful. As Is gets older I'll support her if and when she wants to discuss her inner life with a professional. But first—starting now, as early as possible—I want to give her a set of tools to ride the waves of what Buddhists call the ten thousand joys and ten thousand sorrows, the inevitable ups and downs of life. Tools like Burson's book, with its bright illustrations and school scenarios, will help in the immediate future. Eventually we'll get to more formal instruction around watching the breath and investigating thoughts and emotions to discover their ephemeral nature.

I talk to Kim Tabari, a diversity consultant in Los Angeles who also teaches yoga, about a month after she's introduced meditation to her eleven-year-old son, Azaan. She realized it was time when he frequently began naming frustration as a motivating factor behind his behavior. "What's with all this frustration happening?" she wondered. And so they started doing a guided meditation together every day before school. She finds kid-friendly instruction online and sits with him for anywhere from five to fifteen minutes. He's embraced the practice, even reminding her to sit with him. The keys to success, Tabari says, are flexibility and consistency. She doesn't push him to sit for long periods of time. She started with four minutes and, noting that he was able to be still for that long, gradually increased the sit by two-minute increments. She balks at rigid instruction that implies there's one correct way to meditate. Leaning back into the chair or even lying down can be fine if that's what the body needs, she tells her son. Children crave routine, and a commitment to the practice is important. "I told him that meditation is a lifelong process of tuning into yourself and figuring out what makes you hurt, what makes you smile, what makes you angry, what makes you you. We have to do a little bit of it every day in order to have this overall better health," she tells me. "I try to explain to him as we're doing it that it's not a quick-fix thing."

These aren't Tabari's first conversations with her son about stillness and how the breath can be used to diffuse anger. When he was younger, she weaved these into instruction on movement during yoga sessions she had with him one on one or in classes she offered to Azaan and his peers. A group setting can make the exploration more fun for kids and parents both. Shahara Godfrey, sixty-five, is a meditation teacher in the San Francisco Bay Area who leads such groups. In her work with little ones, she uses activities that take into account the child's desire to have their senses engaged. She'll have kids close their eyes; then she'll strike a bell that emits a full, warm sound that lasts and lasts until it fades away. "When you can't hear the bell anymore, raise your hand," she'll say, delivering a lesson in attention and concentration. For preschool- and kindergarten-age children, she might instruct them to put a hand on their bellies and feel the rise and fall of their breaths or to sit up straight and imagine a string running from the floor through the tops of their heads.

These are simple exercises delivered in small doses that last only minutes, so they're developmentally appropriate even for toddlers. It's important to remember that time moves differently for children, Godfrey tells me. A moment can feel like a lifetime. "I would say to someone who's crying, 'Is this how it's going to be forever?' And the child would nod. 'And ever?' And on and on till the child is laughing," she says. This approach gives a child room to be upset while teaching that emotions aren't static. Joy will inevitably follow sadness, and good times don't last forever. Godfrey gives children room to be honest about however they feel. One group she works with provides space for children to learn together while their parents are in the next room engaged in their own mindfulness practice. Once she has the older children gathered, Godfrey might ask, "How many [of you] really wanted to be here today?" It sounds to me like a good way to encourage kids to remember what they really want, separate from what someone else wants for them. She encourages caregivers to invite self-reflection as well. Say you're reading a child a book that packs an emotional punch or has a tone that evokes a particular feeling. She suggests asking, "How does that make you feel inside?"

"When you address the emotions, you allow a child to be accepting even when it's hard," Godfrey tells me. As she says this, I'm reminded what an awakening it was when, at some point in my thirties, I was taught what's called Buddhism's first noble truth: there is suffering. I still find it profound in its simplicity. Accepting the statement as truth allows life's inevitable shittiness to feel less like a personal affront. Life has hardships, and that's true for everyone. We're certainly allowed to have feelings in response to those hardships, but those feelings won't necessarily change what's happening. I want to give Is age-appropriate lessons in the universality of suffering, the relationship between attachment and suffering, and the tools that help end suffering. By teaching the dharma, Godfrey is offering these lessons in the Bay Area and beyond.

ॐ

MANY OF THE EXERCISES SHE SHARES WITH ME HAPPEN within the family sangha at the East Bay Meditation Center, the same place where I deepened my commitment to Buddhism and meditation beginning in 2009. First, I attended a weekly evening sit for people of color. After a couple of years of this, I attended my first overnight retreat held over MLK weekend at Spirit Rock, a retreat center nearby in Marin County. Soon I decided I was ready to attend my first week-long silent retreat, an endeavor that involves waking at dawn to sit in silence in a cavernous practice hall alongside other practitioners and then moving through a daily rhythm of sitting, walking slowly, and eating in silence. The only talking comes in the form of instruction from teachers seated on a raised platform in the front of the room. They guide practitioners through different kinds of meditation—some focused on watching and releasing what arises in the mind, others focused on cultivating feelings of kindness, joy, forgiveness, or equanimity, a sense of well-being and acceptance. The retreat I attended when I was pregnant with Is was my fourth weeklong immersion in silence and Buddhist teachings.

The culture of these retreats can take some getting used to. The tradition they belong to is called Vipassana, and many of the teachers are Westerners who trained in monasteries in Southeast Asia or India beginning in the 1970s. Digital devices aren't allowed, and participants are encouraged to completely unplug, even in their rooms during rest periods. Eye contact and all nonverbal communication are discouraged, as is journaling or any kind of writing. These suggestions are meant to help participants quiet their minds and let go of any need to explain, react, perform, or make sense of things. From the start, I found these instructions to be incredibly freeing. The quiet, the anonymity, the permission to withdraw inside myself and pause my inner critic suited me. I loved being free to not say or do anything. That first noble truth—that there is suffering—can hit home hard in the midst of the quiet. A lot of difficult emotions, projections, preoccupations, and memories can arise when external stimuli are removed. Sometimes what comes up is tied to experiences of discrimination, exclusion, or other forms of mistreatment. This is why I've found that it feels safer and easier to practice surrounded by seekers and teachers who are of color or at least take seriously the relationship between history, identity, and mindfulness.

There's a short period of time before a retreat officially begins and after it ends when participants are allowed, encouraged even, to talk with one another. It was during this window at one of my first weeklong retreats that I met Christy Leffall, a black Oaklander around my age. She also attended EBMC from time to time and would later go on to join its board. Leffall and I built a friendship over the years and became parents around the same time. Christy and her partner, Gueidi, have a son who is a year older than Is. I'm no longer living in the Bay Area when we get on the phone to talk about our mental and spiritual health in the spring of 2017.

She reflects on the past year and opens up about how tough it's been. She is a gender-queer woman, and the June 2016 mass shooting at the Pulse nightclub—which killed forty-nine people and wounded fifty-three others on a night the Orlando gay bar drew a large Latino crowd—hit her hard. She'd been disturbed by other occurrences on the world stage that summer, including the Brexit vote and the killings of police in Dallas and Baton Rouge that heightened hateful rhetoric against black activists and Black Lives Matter organizing. Election night brought news of a personal tragedy: a family member was shot and killed in his driveway during a robbery. Hours after receiving the news, she learned of Trump's win and cried as she imagined what the new administration might mean for her son, a black and Latino child with two mothers. Leffall and her young family experienced multiple thefts at their apartment and faced a conflict with their landlord as

Bay Area rents skyrocketed. "We were about to be another story of people getting pushed out of their housing over some bullshit."

Her response to the deluge of hard times was to turn inward and enter a period of spiritual soul searching. She abandoned her Facebook account to get away from the constant media chatter that fueled her anxieties. She got honest with herself about her priorities. "I'm just trying to cook a meal and bathe my child and breathe," she tells me. Paying attention to the breath is a fundamental lesson of mindfulness. It happens without our having to do or think about anything. We breathe out fully, trusting that our bodies will automatically take in the next gulp of sustaining oxygen. Letting go, nonattachment, faith—so much wisdom contained in such a simple thing, and quiet time on the cushion allows us to watch it work. "After I meditate, everything opens up," Leffall tells me. "Having a more intentional [sitting] practice has been critical." Leffall sees the relationship between knowing how to take care of herself and knowing how to take care of her son. "My parenting style is driven by what I've already discovered about myself," she says. "Nothing else makes sense if you haven't come to grips with that."

Godfrey, the meditation teacher, has been practicing mindfulness for two decades and is mother to a forty-six-year-old daughter. She tells me that her spiritual orientation often has a calming influence on her relationships with her daughter and two grandchildren, though she doesn't impose her beliefs on them. Instead, they've found comfort in the Christian church, the silence built into Quaker education, an

Afrocentric rites-of-passage program, and elsewhere. Godfrey reflects on meditation and Buddhism as her own "solid
rock," a sustaining force during difficult times. For the past
three years, she's been living with health problems related to
cancer. She spent three months in the hospital, during which
many members of the EBMC and larger Buddhist community rallied around her. She tells me that what she appreciates
about mindfulness is that it's a practice, a calling to consistently apply the philosophy in the world, even and especially
when the world is a painful and inhospitable place. "It's all
interwoven—how I speak, how I engage with people, how
I engage with difficult emotions," she says. "The cushion and
the walking and listening to [dharma] talks, going to retreats
are actually skill-building. But then it's like, 'Well, how do I
live this?'"

Godfrey is my mother's age, and as I listen to the challenges she's navigating with the help of the dharma, I peer
into what my future might look like. She is using her spiritual
practice to decide how to best support her daughter and
grandchildren, how to deal with recurring cancer and related
ailments she'll have for the rest of her life. As the single parent
of a young child, I need to think of my own spiritual practice in new ways. I'm not sure how to calmly manage the big
questions in my own life when the skills-building exercises
that I've relied on for nearly a decade—sitting and walking
meditation and going on retreat—feel nearly impossible now
that I have a toddler to care for.

A conversation with a dear friend who is mother to toddler
twins and practices mindfulness after a childhood in church

helps me see that, practically speaking, Christianity has a leg up on Buddhism when it comes to welcoming families with young children. My mom sat in the pews during Sunday services, children's choir performances, and Christmas pageants occasionally but not always. There was infrastructure so that I could participate independent of adult family members. As a child, there was a place for me, and it was a place that offered celebration and fun. Not so in most meditation centers, which are focused on silence and introspection. This is certainly the focus at the Cincinnati center where I was first introduced to the dharma and which is a few blocks from where Is and I now live. I've gone alone a couple of times since moving back home a few years ago, but after years of connection to Buddhism in the Bay Area, the options in my hometown lack diversity in race and age. There are too few opportunities to build community that acknowledges the social and political battles raging in the world outside its walls.

For something akin to what I want for my family now, I turn again to EBMC, where Michele Ku started dreaming up a family sangha back in 2007. Ku, a Chinese American mother of one, had been a longtime meditator before she became a mom. Like me, she'd been on retreat at Spirit Rock and Insight Meditation Society. "I had no place to go with my child," she tells me of her search for spiritual community as she transitioned to parenthood. "I didn't go on retreat. I didn't go to meditation centers. It was clear to me: this is so isolating."

Eleven years ago, she and her husband took their daughter cross-country to a family retreat at IMS outside Boston.

At four, their child just made the minimum age requirement for kids. The experience was beneficial, but Ku was struck by how white the retreat was. Out of more than one hundred people in attendance, theirs was one of three Asian families. She noticed just a few families of color in all. While she was there, she had a vision: she needed to build a diverse family sangha, a spiritual community that was safe and inviting for families of color, multiracial families, and LGBTQ families. That same year, she started organizing with three other families, and they started meeting outside at local parks. EBMC had just opened its doors and was located in a small storefront in downtown Oakland that couldn't accommodate the group. She completed a training program at nearby Spirit Rock Meditation Center that gave her the tools to build the sangha and connected her to others who could help.

She knew that unlike other family mindfulness communities she'd encountered, hers would welcome people with babies and toddlers. A nursing mom or the parent of a rambunctious two-year-old shouldn't be shunned, she decided. Instead, the point was to help parents drop the judgment, the comparing, the guilt and self-blame that can plague so many of us when we become responsible for shepherding a new person through life. Teachers in EBMC's family sangha (Godfrey is among them) ask parents to simply notice how they're feeling during gatherings rather than trying to change those feelings or strive for some performance of perfection. They talk about how to bring mindfulness and patience into time spent with their children. They make sure adults know of free resources they can use to stay connected to the practice now that they're short on time and money, apps that can guide even a quick five-minute sit, and a website that offers renowned teachers' retreat talks to the public free of charge.

In building the sangha, Ku and others have maintained their goal of creating a refuge for families of color. She acknowledges that there are Buddhist temples in the Bay Area that cater to the Asian immigrant communities that brought the religion with them to the United States. In her experience, those wouldn't have worked for her family. "I found it too restrictive, especially for my daughter when she was little," Ku says of her experience visiting a Japanese American temple. "I didn't want to turn her away from something because it was rigid." The community she's helped build over the past decade is thriving, with between fifty and sixty people showing up to monthly gatherings and families clamoring for more frequent meet-ups. They ensure inclusivity by making sure the group that assembles is made up of at least 50 percent people of color. People are asked about various aspects of their identity, including race, when they register. If too many white people register, they're put on a waitlist in an effort to maintain a balance, Ku explains. Some may bristle at EBMC's explicit use of racial quotas, but Ku says it creates the container they need for the types of conversations that come up. One white father of biracial children wondered aloud recently how he can protect his children. "I think he'd never thought about it before Trump," Ku tells me. She also shares that a black parent of a five-year-old asked of a teacher, "What do I do when my daughter asks, 'Do all white people hate us, Mommy?'"

Especially in this political and cultural moment, families need a place to be honest about the events that rock them. After the October 2017 mass shooting in Las Vegas, a mother shared how she had talked about the tragedy with her daughter. "One person did this, and hundreds of people stayed and helped," Ku says, relaying that parent's message to her child. The sangha's teachers and participants remind each other of the central tenets of Buddhism—loving-kindness, generosity, compassion, truthful speech. "All the things that are no longer being practiced by our government," Ku says. "Now we have an oppressive government that functions out of greed, hatred, and delusion. The dharma's the major guiding sanity in an insane world."

As Is grows, I want her to be able to find sanity in the midst of chaos. I also want her to feel a connection to the sacred, that which has the power to transform us and which reaches us from somewhere beyond the intellectual. I find this for myself in a number of ways. Meditation is one way. I can hear a song Mrs. Ramseur, our church pianist and my beloved babysitter, played three decades ago and be transported someplace that feels both grounded in the present and otherworldly. I have sometimes touched into this sense of the sacred through politics as well.

In the spring of 2017, I am at my desk watching a press conference streamed live from Raleigh, North Carolina. I have written about Rev. William Barber and the Moral Mondays movement that built a multiracial coalition to challenge the Republican takeover of the state's government. On this particular morning, Barber and others are announcing the launch of a national poor people's campaign. One by one, leaders in North Carolina progressive politics—some of whom I've interviewed—share what they've accomplished together, including engaging in sustained civil disobedience in the statehouse and surviving mass arrests in the summer of 2013 and organizing against a voter suppression law targeting black voters that was eventually struck down in the courts.[1] In their short remarks, the speakers seem genuinely appreciative and supportive of each other. I remember how, during a weeklong reporting trip to North Carolina, I'd observe activists chant "Thank you! We love you!" again and again after someone had done a brave thing or shared something personal that was difficult but reflective of broader community struggles. Sitting at my desk that morning, I started to cry. The North Carolinians' efforts communicated a righteousness, a certainty that their path was the right one and that it was blessed by something much bigger than themselves and that couldn't be explained simply through policy arguments.

I was moved to tears in part because those North Carolina activists were saying to one another, "I see you" and "You matter." It's not often in life that others hold up a mirror so that we can see ourselves clearly, see where we've been and where we're going. I want this for our family, but Joan Halifax, an anthropologist and Buddhist teacher, notes how rare such opportunities are for most of us in the United States. In a 2012 interview, Halifax said, "When a baby is born, [there's] usually no real rite of passage that sacralizes an individual's life. When an individual encounters their puberty, where our identity changes in a really extraordinary way, again, there's nothing to mark that change in the lives of most of our young people."[2] After observing the Dogon people of Mali engage in a rite-of-passage ceremony that engages the entire culture and happens once every fifty-three years, Halifax asked herself, "What in my world, what in my country, allows us to mature?"

Halifax and other white Americans might be most familiar with bar and bat mitzvahs and *quinceañeras* as coming-of-age rituals brought to this country by immigrants. When I was growing up, I heard a bit about African-centered rites-of-passage programs for black preteens but never participated in one. Beginning in the late 1960s, many black American communities developed initiation programs to help prepare young people for adulthood.[3] G. Rosaline Preudhomme, the seventy-three-year-old mother and grandmother in New York City, implemented such programs in Detroit, New York, Philadelphia, Toronto, and Miami in the 1990s and early 2000s. The model she developed was adapted from the seven principles of Nguzo Saba, the Swahili-named philosophy outlined by Maulana Karenga, the creator of Kwanzaa. These principles are unity, self-determination, collective work and responsibility, cooperative economics, purpose, creativity, and faith. In Preudhomme's view, training black youth in Afrocentric traditions and culture is necessary in the diaspora. "We've been scattered everywhere," she says. "We are always in search of the groups that really rooted us." The programs she ran encouraged participants' self-esteem and emphasized that each individual has a contribution to make to the larger community. "It's a journey that reminds young people of their greatness," she says.

These programs aren't as popular today as they were two decades ago. But Shahara Godfrey, the EBMC teacher who helps lead the family sangha, mentions that when her grandchildren were younger, they went through a rites-of-passage program at the progressive Atlanta-area church they attended. She applauded her daughter for giving her grandchildren an opportunity to gather with other young black people to explore questions around values and history and their futures. "The same tenets that they were talking about in terms of moral inventory and knowledge of self is the dharma." She's right. There's overlap in many of these traditions. Now my challenge is to find or create the community where our family can feel welcome, seen in all our complexities, and lovingly held as we try to better know ourselves.

CHAPTER 9

Power

WHEN SHE IS THREE MONTHS OLD, MY DAUGHTER TAKES HER FIRST flight. She and my mom come with me to a health-care conference in Orlando, where I'm gathering information for a story on maternal health. When she is five months old, she and my mom hit the streets with me on a chilly January day to cover Cincinnati's women's march. I snap photos of protest signs and talk to some of the thousands of people who have turned out to protest Trump's inauguration. The next month, my mom and daughter accompany me to Santa Fe, where I give a talk at an event hosted by a local women's foundation. I have taken the first three months of her life off work, but as soon as I'm back at it, Is is by my side and my own mother is with us, supporting us so that I can breastfeed and keep my girl close. At this stage in her life, my daughter is unaware of what I'm doing, content to spend time with her grandmother while I'm working. But soon enough, she'll ask questions, and I'll share with her what I'm up to. This is one way I'll pass on an understanding of politics, power, and organizing to my daughter. I will share with her the stories that I collect and tell her why they're significant.

The summer before Is turns two, the three of us are on the road again, this time to the San Francisco Bay Area, where I hope to learn what politically oriented mothering looks like for others and how they pass their values on to their children. I'm lucky to catch Cat Brooks during the trip. In addition to running for mayor of Oakland, the organizer is on the move. She's just back from a people's filibuster in Washington, DC, demanding that the government reunify the families it separated at the US-Mexico border. Before that, she was in San Diego in support of an action calling for the abolition of ICE. Immigration is on the front burner in the summer of 2018, given the media spotlight on the Trump administration's policies, but Brooks has been challenging state violence for years. The killing of Oscar Grant by a transit police officer in January 2009 thrust her to the center of Oakland politics and solidified her place as one of the nation's most visible black liberation movement leaders. In 2014 she cofounded the Anti-Police Terror Project, an organization that supports the families of people killed or violated by police.

On this July afternoon, we're in her office in downtown Oakland, where the walls are covered with posters demanding justice for Aiyana Stanley-Jones, Alan Blueford, and others slain by police. On a desk is a framed photo of Brooks and her now twelve-year-old daughter, Jadyn, beaming at the camera. The picture was taken Mother's Day 2017 when the girl saved enough money to rent a limo and take Brooks out for dinner at the Cheesecake Factory. Brooks doesn't take moments like these—outings that are just about family, fun, and celebration—for granted. She and Jadyn often have to sacrifice downtime in favor of addressing some pressing community need. "You see these families, and every weekend they're going hiking, or they have dinner together every night, and then they watch TV. That's not our reality," she says of her family. "We have to be in meetings and in the streets. So it's a balancing act unlike what I think other folks have to engage in."

Brooks is talking about her own life, but she's also talking about the particular demands of black motherhood as she sees them. Black mothering is a political project, and our mission—should we choose to accept it—is nothing short of revolutionary. "Our job as black mothers is to keep pushing the liberation ball down the court. Our obligation is to leave the world better for them and to ensure that they are equipped with the tools that they need to fight. We don't have the luxury of living normal lives," Brooks says. "I tell my daughter all the time—and it's harsh—but we don't live for the I. We live for the we."

Twenty-five years ago, scholar Patricia Hill Collins coined the term "motherwork" to describe the political project Brooks alludes to. At the time, most white, middle-class feminist theorizing about motherhood focused on oppression *within* the home. Mothers were assumed to be unemployed and confined to the domestic sphere, thus dependent on a male patriarch whose earning power kept the family afloat. In her essay "Shifting the Center: Race, Class, and Feminist Theorizing about Motherhood," Collins upended this portrayal. Instead, she wrote, mothers of color often worked outside the home, and the domestic labor they performed was seen as part of the family's overall uplift effort rather than something exploitative. For mothers of color, she wrote, "'Reproductive labor' or 'motherwork' goes beyond ensuring the survival of members of one's family. This type of motherwork recognizes that individual survival, empowerment, and identity require group survival, empowerment, and identity."[1]

Black mothers advocate for our children everywhere, from the playground to the schoolhouse to the doctor's office. There is always a campaign to wage. There is always a need to make our children's humanity more visible and to convince, cajole, or pressure someone who's making our lives more difficult because of their own blind spots or racist impulses. Activism is woven into the fabric of our daily lives, and it doesn't take long before we see the systemic reasons we're constantly waging these campaigns on behalf of our own children and families. That's when we start connecting the dots between our struggles and others' and, as Brooks puts it, start living for the we.

The election of Donald Trump has raised the stakes. Already we've seen the impact of a Trump presidency in cahoots with a Republican-controlled Congress and a conservative majority on the Supreme Court. Upon taking office, the president immediately waged war on nonwhite immigrants, Muslims, and the poor. His appointments to the Supreme Court are likely to be hostile to voting rights, workers' rights, and protections against housing and employment discrimination. His administration wants to undermine low-income women's ability to terminate a pregnancy or get birth control.

Such restrictions threaten all women and especially black women, who have relatively high abortion rates because we are disproportionately poor and lack access to health care.

As if policy assaults weren't enough, Trump has fostered antiblack rhetoric in public discourse. He blamed "both sides" for the violence that gripped Charlottesville in the summer of 2017 after white supremacists marched in the streets. He regularly refers to black public figures and journalists as "stupid" and "crazy" and otherwise demeans them. In his view, Haiti, El Salvador, and African nations are "shithole countries." Any black football player who kneels during the national anthem to protest state violence is a "son of a bitch." News about the scandals, the trials, and the investigations related to the Trump campaign and administration breaks daily if not hourly, and what we know as American democracy is coming apart at the seams. Black mothers—already up to our elbows in motherwork—are being asked to resist, to clean up a mess we saw coming a mile away.

Ninety-four percent of black women cast their ballots against Trump in 2016. No other demographic so resolutely closed ranks in an effort to avert his presidency. But despite many black women's best efforts in advance of the election, we collectively were Cassandra, our warnings disbelieved and dismissed by the larger electorate. It would be nice to indulge in fantasies of leaving the country, as some have done since the election. But as one black mother, who once moved her family to Brazil for eight years, reminded me, "Antiblack racism is deeply rooted everywhere." When I imagine whisking Is away to some improved reality, I struggle and fail to think of a place where black women and girls can be safe, respected as equals, allowed to simply be human. A *New Yorker* profile of the Nigerian writer Chimamanda Ngozi Adichie addresses my quandary. Larissa MacFarquhar writes of Ngozi Adichie's musings on where to raise her own two-year-old daughter:

> She wants to raise her child in Nigeria, because she wants her to be protected as she herself was protected, growing up there: not knowing she is black. Someday she will talk to her about what it means to be black, but not yet. She wants her daughter to be in a place where race as she has encountered it in America does not exist . . . On the other hand, raising her daughter in Nigeria would mean that she would likely learn much sooner, and more definitively than she would in America, that she was a girl. She doesn't want her to know that too early, either.[2]

I've only visited a handful of countries on the African continent. My longest stay was in Ghana, as a college student, for five months. But I can slip into romanticizing Africa and the Caribbean, places where black people are in the majority and in leadership. Of course I long for an escape hatch in times like these. Knowing I don't have one makes me even more curious about how people like Cat Brooks are coping in today's climate. When you've devoted your adult life to organizing in defense of black communities and then someone like Trump comes along and turns the heat up even higher, what do you do?

For many of the mothers I speak with, they are doing what they've always done—continuing to educate and organize—but with a new urgency or in slightly different venues. For Brooks, this has meant a pivot toward electoral politics. As a vocal opponent of police violence and former host of a popular local radio show, Brooks has been a visible community leader in Oakland for the past decade. She is a member of the Black Lives Matter Bay Area chapter and was one of the Black Friday 14, a group of black activists who protested state violence in November 2014 by chaining themselves to a commuter train and shutting down the Bay Area Rapid Transit system on the busiest shopping day of the year.[3]

At the launch of her mayoral campaign in May 2018, Brooks told the crowd of four hundred people that until recently she'd never had any interest in electoral politics. "I like being in the streets with the people. I like grassroots organizing," she said. But, she continued, it may be time to fight from inside city hall given the challenges facing Oaklanders: a child sex-abuse scandal in the police department, massive development projects that ignore the existing communities' needs, and a housing crisis brought on by an influx of high-income tech workers from San Francisco and Silicon Valley. Oakland, birthplace of the Black Panther Party, has lost nearly a third of its black population since 2000. The city was once 47 percent black.[4]

Brooks kept coming back to the power of community organizing to offer hope to those gathered. After all, she says, street protest and mass mobilization have changed the conversation, from demanding more transparent city budgeting to securing charges against the police officers accused of sexually assaulting and trafficking a teenager. "We have always been the vanguard of resistance in this country," she told the Oakland crowd. Now Brooks is seeking an even bigger platform from which to lead. As she sees it, the Trump era offers an important opportunity for solutions-oriented left activists and organizers to make major strides with the broader public. She recalls being at an all-black bar in Oakland watching election results come in that November night in 2008 when Barack Obama won his first term. When enough states had gone blue to ensure that McCain had no shot at the presidency, the bar's patrons started singing the Negro spiritual "Free at Last." Brooks turned to her husband and said, "We're fucked."

In her view, Obama's presidency lulled even some of the most dogged skeptics into a false sense of security. Die-hard conservatives and racists may have been outraged by his administration, but the rest of us were too busy congratulating ourselves on having reached a historic milestone to stay vigilant. With Trump in office that's changed, Brooks says, and she's ready to take advantage of the moment. Now even those who never really understood all the fuss about immigration policy or police violence are so horrified by Trumpism that they're ready to fight. By engaging with people who have long been in the struggle, newcomers to organizing might wake up to the contradictions that have been here all along. "They're like, 'No, we're not that. That is not America,'" Brooks tells me, paraphrasing what she hears from those shocked and outraged by Trump. "We're like, 'Yeah, it is, but I don't even need to have that fight with you right now. We can talk about that after we win.'" The ideas that Brooks and others like her have long advocated—investing public dollars in policies that keep people educated, housed, and fed rather than investing in police departments, jails, and prisons, for example—are finding more receptive audiences. "This makes more sense in the face of something so crazy," she says. Brooks doesn't think change will happen overnight, but she's willing to jump into electoral politics to see if she can amplify antiracist, left demands as Oakland's mayor.

The timing may be especially good for Brooks, since the Trump era has created among progressives a new appreciation for black women's role in electoral politics. There's finally widespread acknowledgment that black women are the single most loyal Democratic voting bloc, and not as passive party followers but as key strategists, communicators, and engines of turnout in their communities. In the 2017 Alabama Senate race that drew national attention because of the sexual abuse allegations against then incumbent Republican Roy Moore, white women overwhelmingly backed Moore. Ninety-eight percent of black women voters in Alabama supported Democratic candidate Doug Jones, who won the seat. There's a new energy around black women politicians and candidates as well. "Auntie" Maxine Waters and Kamala Harris are progressive movement heroes whose truth-telling channels the skepticism and rage of so many. With her campaign to become Georgia's governor, and the first black woman in the nation to serve in that role, Stacey Abrams came closer to a win than any Democrat in the state in almost two decades. While many have noted the role of the GOP's voter suppression tactics in keeping Abrams from the governor's mansion, she has said she's likely to run again or to seek a US Senate seat.[5]

In July 2018, Lucy McBath won the Democratic nomination in Georgia's Sixth Congressional District and in November defeated the Republican incumbent. McBath is the mother of Jordan Davis, who in 2012 was shot and killed at a Florida gas station by a forty-five-year-old white man who instigated a dispute with seventeen-year-old Davis and Davis's friends over the volume of their music. In the wake of the tragedy, McBath has become an advocate against gun violence and is part of what's called the "Mothers of the Movement," black mothers of children who died during police interactions or at the hands of white vigilantes. She now regularly connects her personal devastation to its political significance, as she did when she endorsed Hillary Clinton from the stage at the Democratic National Convention in 2016:

> You don't stop being a parent when your child dies. I am still Jordan Davis's mother. His life ended the day he was shot and killed for playing loud music. But my job as his mother didn't. I still wake up every day thinking about how to parent him. How to protect him and his legacy. How to ensure his death doesn't overshadow his life . . . I lived in fear my son would die like this. I even warned him that because he was a young, black man, he would meet people who didn't value his life. That is a conversation no parent should ever have to have.[6]

McBath's own child is gone, but she is now advocating for gun control reform through the organizations Everytown for Gun Safety and Moms Demand Action for Gun Sense in America.

She sees changing gun laws as an extension of her work mothering Jordan. "Championing for them in Washington is still championing for my child, I'm still a mother, I'm still parenting," she has said.[7] McBath's and Brooks's campaigns faced long odds. McBath's district hadn't elected a Democrat to Congress since the 1970s, and the seat was once held by Newt Gingrich, an architect of the conservative Contract with America. In the end, Brooks couldn't oust incumbent mayor Libby Schaaf, who took 57.1 percent of the vote compared to Brooks's 22.3 percent. But McBath and Brooks are both part of a trend that has more women and people of color running for office in recent years. *Mother Jones's* Jamilah King has reported that 2,400 women—more than 300 of whom are women of color—have participated in Emily's List trainings for pro-choice Democratic women since Trump's election. That's up from 920 women participants in 2016. Between 2012 and 2018, there was a 75 percent increase in the number of women of color running for Congress and for state legislatures, according to one recent report.[8]

I love that more black women are running for office as a way of scaling up their motherwork or efforts to better their own families' lives by trying to ensure survival and empowerment for a larger group. I also know that we don't all aspire to a seat in Congress or on a school board or county commission. For the past twenty years, I've been engaged in public service in some way, most often by researching what matters most to me and then informing as many people as I can through writing or teaching. I've been motivated by the belief that information changes hearts and minds and moves people to act. But since becoming a mother, what I feel is a desire to get quiet, scale back, and focus on work with an impact I can see immediately and over which I feel more control.

I've entered motherhood just as Trumpism has made the world look especially bleak. The stakes feel higher than ever before in my lifetime just as my energy and optimism are flagging. I hear and appreciate Brooks's analysis about the opportunity of the current moment, but the electorate is fickle, and the cracks in our democratic institutions are becoming more obvious. Even when we overcome voter disenfranchisement and the Electoral College to elect people who share our values, any progressive policies they put in place can be easily overturned. All it takes is a reactionary wave of public sentiment (sometimes aided by the meddling of a foreign power) to sweep new leaders into office. These days I want to know that I can keep my daughter safe no matter what comes our way, including the breakdown of the institutions and social structures we've come to take for granted.

I feel less alone in my apocalyptic thoughts after I talk to Zahra Alabanza. Alabanza was working in Chicago when she got sick with a chronic illness. The diagnosis came just as she was thinking big picture about her career, which involved teaching social work at a local university and advocating for reproductive health services for teenagers.

Exhausted and burned out, Alabanza realized that though she wanted her work to bring positive change to communities, she wasn't living out the values she espoused. And it wasn't an individual failing on her part. It was a contradiction she saw playing out all around her. From her vantage point, social justice organizers' politics often weren't aligned with their actual lives. Something clicked. "I need to slow down and do something different," she remembers thinking. She saved $20,000 over six months and headed south with her boys to Atlanta. She planned to do three things once settled there: grow food, ride a bike, and do yoga.

Over time, what were initially practices she used to heal herself became political projects. Becoming certified in permaculture design and sustainable urban agriculture led her to like-minded community and built confidence in her ability to survive a worst-case scenario. "When the world ends, I can grow my own food," she tells me, or at least organize a team that could produce enough to live on. Training her body to bike for hundreds of miles, taking her sons on long bike trips and backcountry hiking, and practicing enough yoga to become a teacher has also made Alabanza feel more secure. "If I need to flee a space, I know my body is physically able because I can ride a bike really far," she tells me. "If I need to carry my children, I can do that."

I am often embarrassed by my growing desire to abandon petitioning the state or amplifying the work of those who do in favor of concentrating my efforts on the health and well-being of my inner circle of family and friends, at least for as long as the earth can sustain us. That's selfish, fear-based thinking, I tell myself. The Bundy family rejecting the authority of the federal government on western public lands and forcing an armed standoff represents this kind of cynical and absurd thinking. The superrich stockpiling generators and ammunition and buying up land in New Zealand represent this kind of every-man-for-himself thinking.[9] But when Alabanza tells me, "We can create the world we want to live in in a micro way," I see that she is engaged in the type of political work that speaks to me more and more. I wonder if her family is proof that we can take on the powers that be by simply making ourselves less vulnerable to their whims.

These days, creating the world we want to live in has to include limiting the flow of information that our children are exposed to. I think deeply about the unprecedented power of digital media after I speak with Monifa Bandele, a mother and organizer living in Brooklyn. Bandele challenges my assertion that the Trump era represents something new. Instead, she says, what's been new in recent years is the speed and ease with which white supremacist violence and rhetoric reach young people. "We had to wait till the evening news to watch the Rodney King beating again," she tells me. "But our children watched Eric Garner take his last breath over and over again." On tiny screens, young people have watched twelve-year-old Tamir Rice, sixteen-year-old Laquan McDonald—children their own ages—be executed. Parents sometimes don't even know that they need to intervene, let alone how to.

We can't yet know the effects that access to digital media showing police killings and acts of racially motivated violence and humiliation are having on young people. So far, the data don't look good. Psychologist Jean Twenge has found that beginning in 2012, rates of teen depression, anxiety, and suicide have gone through the roof. This is around the same time a majority of Americans came to own smartphones. Twenge has said that iGen—the term she uses to describe

young people born between 1995 and 2012—are "on the
brink of the worst mental-health crisis in decades," and she
links the coming crisis to the time they spend on electronic
devices.[10]

Sometimes the content of what young people witness
on their phones is traumatizing; other times it's the sheer
volume of interaction that's overwhelming. Bandele and her
husband, Lumumba, have considered different ways to help
their daughters navigate all the information and images that
reach them through their phones, from group chat messages to social media. She's realized that simply saying "no
screens" doesn't work. "Screens are like paper now," she says.
They're ubiquitous from the high school classroom to the
laptops where young people are often expected to do their
homework. What's worked so far has been encouraging
her daughters to take breaks. Bandele once took her older
daughter's phone overnight in an effort to enforce some
downtime. She put the phone on silent and went to bed. In
the morning the girl had received more than three hundred
notifications from a group chat with kids from school. Some
conflict had jumped off the day before, and the young people had spent the hours between 11:00 p.m. and 6:00 a.m.
in conversation about it, pregaming whatever in-person
interaction would take place the next day. If nothing else,
the girl would have been tired from participating in the conversation all night.

Technology that amplifies the messages and cultural climate of the Trump era—not necessarily Trump himself—has
created a new battleground on which black parents must work

to protect and support their children, Bandele says. Enforcing mental health breaks is now part of our motherwork as well.

ॐ

MARGARET PRESCOD, AN LA-BASED ACTIVIST AND RADIO host, began to develop her analysis of power as a child growing up in Barbados. That's when she noticed the gap between what was expected of girls and what was expected of boys. There was always ironing, cleaning, or other housework for her or her older sister to do. But her brother never had to scrub the floors or take food to the neighbor. In the village where Prescod grew up, women ran the households. They cooked the food, took care of the children, and managed the money.

She later immigrated to the United States and in her early twenties taught at an elementary school in Ocean Hill–Brownsville. It was the late 1960s, and a historic fight for community control of schools was underway in this low-income Brooklyn neighborhood. Prescod saw that it was black mothers—many of them factory workers, maids, or on welfare—who led the organizing effort to ensure that if the school would not be integrated, then its teachers and administrators would be black or of color just like the student body. She then taught at Queens College during the fight for open admissions to the City University of New York (CUNY), which from 1970 to 1976 made all New York City high school graduates eligible for admission to one of CUNY's seventeen campuses. The policy change ushered in thousands of low-income black and Latino students who otherwise would not have had access to higher education.[11] Prescod saw once again that poor women advocating fiercely on their children's behalf were the key to a successful campaign. "I got a whole education in who mothers on welfare were and their contributions in low-income communities, because they were the ones there holding things down," she tells me. Sadly, their leadership too often went unacknowledged, and the stereotype of the lazy, do-nothing welfare mother persisted.

Prescod soon found an organizing home in the Brooklyn chapter of the Wages for Housework Campaign, an international organization that advanced the idea that women should be paid for domestic labor. Her work demanding rights for families on welfare deepened, and in 1977 she helped shape the plan of action that came out of the first and only National Women's Conference, which was funded by Congress and drew tens of thousands of women to Houston. Working alongside the National Welfare Rights Organization, Prescod and other black women in Wages for Housework opposed workfare (which would end up as the backbone of welfare reform in 1996) and successfully fought to include a line in the platform that read, "Just as with other workers, homemakers receiving income transfer payments should be afforded the dignity of having that payment called a wage, not welfare."[12]

By the mid-1980s, Prescod was living in Los Angeles and had a toddler daughter. She had stopped teaching when her child was born and became what she calls "a full-time mom and a full-time activist." By then she had a new focus: dozens of black women had been found dead in South Central

Los Angeles, apparently killed by the same man, but the LAPD was refusing to seriously investigate. Prescod told NPR that when she and a group of friends went to police headquarters to learn more, the police captain asked them, "Why are you concerned about it? He's only killing hookers."[13] She founded an organization called the Black Coalition Fighting Back Serial Murders and publicly pressured the police force—which had labeled the crimes "no humans involved"—over three decades. In 2016, the serial killer known as the Grim Sleeper was convicted of killing nine women and a teenage girl between 1985 and 2007 and sentenced to death. Many credit Prescod for raising the alarm and forcing reluctant police and prosecutors to pursue justice for a community they were otherwise happy to ignore.

Prescod has spent nearly five decades speaking truth to power, and she's open about the toll it has taken. She shares her political history with ease but emphasizes that she doesn't want to sugarcoat things. "I was also stressed out," she tells me. "I was a low-income, single mother trying to organize and also be a mother, and I think that children pick up on stress." In the course of fighting for some of the country's most marginalized women—welfare mothers and sex workers—she has had to worry about her family's safety. When her daughter was young, Prescod received threats, and on separate occasions found someone menacing parked outside her house and a dead bird hung outside her window. She took small steps to maintain a sense of safety and normalcy. She made sure someone knew where she was at all times. She got a bodyguard and a big dog. She drove her daughter to and from the school bus stop and hung blankets in her home's bay windows to protect the family's privacy.

But she still thinks back on decisions she made that affected her daughter, Chanda Prescod-Weinstein, an academic who, according to 2015 data, is the nation's only black woman working in theoretical astrophysics and the sixty-third black American woman to earn a PhD in physics. Prescod sometimes still wonders whether, after she and her daughter's father split, she should have moved with the girl back east to be closer to Prescod's family. She second-guesses her decision to not take her daughter with her to the World Conference on Women in Beijing in 1995. A preteen Prescod-Weinstein had really wanted to go, but Prescod said no, certain that she'd be working too intensely on getting a resolution valuing unpaid work included in the platform. A decade later, in 2005 after Hurricane Katrina hit the Gulf Coast, Prescod decided to go to New Orleans to support those affected at the same time her daughter was moving house and had asked for help.

Prescod thinks of all the ways her daughter has had to share her with a wider community. "As a mother, you always carry so much guilt," she tells me. But in her view the key is to apologize when necessary and to talk about hard things head on. "We've had some difficult but productive conversations. You kind of become better people because of it." Prescod-Weinstein apparently understands the choices her mother has made. In 2015 she told an interviewer, "My mom was singlehandedly the strongest influence in terms of understanding the sacrifices people make for those that they love and for the communities that they cherish."[14]

It seems the price of engaging in motherwork is the possibility that your child will think you focused too much on beating back the threats of the outside world and not enough on the smaller family unit. Cat Brooks wonders how her daughter, now twelve, will look back on these days, when meetings and rallies and protests are such a central part of the time they spend together. After Oscar Grant was killed by BART police at the start of 2009, Brooks, who is also a performer, wrote a poem called "For Oscar" that reads in part: "How do I explain to my 3-year-old why I'm marching in the street? How do I explain to my 3-year-old why she ain't seen me all week? How do I explain to my 3-year-old what his death has done to me?"[15] Around that same time, Brooks sent an Oscar Grant T-shirt to Jadyn, who was spending a summer with her grandmother in Las Vegas. The little girl refused to put on the T-shirt and told her grandmother, "I hate Oscar Grant. He took my mommy away."[16]

Nine years later, life is still fast-paced, and Brooks is still supporting the families of people killed by police in addition to running for mayor. She tears up a little when I ask her how she responded to her daughter's frustration back then and whether she still sees it today. "I don't know if I did it the right way. I don't know if I've been selfish. I'm sure sometimes I have. I know I have not always placed my family first," she tells me. "And we're *dying*. For whatever reason, this is what the ancestors call me to do. It hurts. I'm not callous about it. It just is what it is."

Having a preteen is tough, she tells me. She knows that soon she'll have a bona fide teenager who will be even more independent. But Brooks has moments of deep pride when she sees the benefit of raising her daughter the way she is. She tells me that just the night before our conversation, Jadyn was telling her about a squabble she'd gotten into on Instagram. The girl had tried to explain to some detractors that while police abolition might not be possible today, working toward making police obsolete is a worthy goal. Brooks's eyes widened with excitement. "And she's twelve!" she reminds me. "I was like, 'You might be mad at me when you're twenty because we didn't spend enough time, but OK. I'm doing my job.'"

Bandele, the Brooklyn-based mother of nineteen- and sixteen-year-old daughters, and her husband have let their own experiences growing up in activist homes shape how they've decided to pass on political values to their children. Bandele's father had been active in the Black Panther Party in the 1960s, and her father and in-laws were part of a movement that built independent African-centered schools in New York City and nationwide throughout the 1970s and 1980s. An uncle was part of the national movement to secure reparations for African descendants. When she thinks back on her childhood, she remembers the adults in her life out in the streets protesting and going to meetings. They were engaged in the movement to end apartheid in South Africa. Black talk radio forms the soundtrack of some childhood memories. The concerns of the world and the self-determination of black people were central to her life. "I loved it," she tells me but emphasizes that hers is just one experience. "I talk to my peers whose parents were even more on the front lines and they're like, 'My house got raided when I was a kid, and I have PTSD, and I'm mad about that.'"

When the state views a people-powered challenge to be a serious threat, the blowback can be tremendous. Bandele lists the ways that growing up in an activist family can traumatize a child: In 1977, black liberation activist Assata Shakur was convicted of murdering a New Jersey state trooper. Her supporters maintain that she is innocent and was targeted by law enforcement because of her political activity. When Shakur escaped from prison in 1979, the police raided the school Bandele's husband attended. Tanks once rolled up to the Mississippi home where Bandele's friend, a child at the time, was staying with her family. Bandele's sister-in-law keeps away from rallies even now: As a child, she and her little brother had been at an anti-apartheid demonstration where mounted police charged their horses into the crowd. "It took her a long time to process, 'Why would my parents put me in danger?'" Bandele says. It's difficult for a child to understand the larger political importance of what's happening around them when they're overwhelmed by a visceral experience of fear, uncertainty, or sadness. Some friends are just now reconnecting with parents who were imprisoned for decades because of their political activity, she says.

Bandele and her husband decided to be sure movement work never came before family. "We're very intentional about making sure our children know that they are the most important thing to us," she says. That's meant not forcing their daughters to go to meetings or rallies and being selective even when historic events are unfolding right on their doorstep. They did take the girls to the Occupy Wall Street encampment, but on a day specifically geared toward children's participation. Bandele's husband was involved in organizing in the wake of the Ferguson protests of 2014 and frequently traveled to the Missouri town. But he never took his daughters with him. The risks could've become too great, Bandele says, and even when adults think they can manage those risks, they never know how the child might look back and perceive the experience. "What you think you're exposing them to and what you're actually exposing them to sometimes are two different things," she says.

Instead of demanding that their daughters be present at various sites of resistance, the Bandeles have focused on instilling in their daughters a key value: "You have to act on injustice." As the girls have gotten older, they've decided how to respond to the world around them. Bandele's oldest daughter was thirteen when self-appointed neighborhood watchman George Zimmerman killed seventeen-year-old Trayvon Martin. Her response was informed by the political struggle she'd seen her parents engaged in. "She was active with her friends," Bandele says. "They protested in school. They protested outside of school. To this day, her voicemail still says, 'Rest in peace, Trayvon Martin.'"

Bandele emphasizes that different children will make sense of the world in different ways. Some will process with relative ease the inescapable traumas of growing up black and needing to stay engaged in resisting political and cultural oppression. Others will fold under the weight of it all.

But for activist adults, sheltering one's children isn't really an option. "When our kids were coming up, we made an effort to create a space that was separate from the activism," she tells me. "At the end of the day, it doesn't work. You can't separate what's going on in the outside world from your home and your kids."

In talking with these mothers who have made it their business to challenge powerful institutions, I wonder how I'll pass on my values to my daughter. Sure, Is can sometimes come with me when I report, especially if my own mother continues to be such a major source of support. But usually the conversations that make up the bulk of my work happen over the phone or at times that I've arranged childcare so that I can attend that protest or conference or meet with a source. So much of the political education the mothers I speak to describe as having shaped their children has happened in real time, with their young ones tagging along and learning by osmosis. Dream hampton, a writer and founding member of the New York chapter of Malcolm X Grassroots Movement, says of her now twenty-three-year-old daughter, Nina, "She was the movement baby falling asleep in the meeting. I don't think I told her what organizing was; she just saw it."

I hear the same thing from Brooks, who describes the people with whom she organizes as her daughter's second family, and from Prescod, who recalls pushing a three-month-old Chanda in a stroller while she passed out leaflets. When she was older, the girl helped pass around sign-in lists at meetings or worked on art projects with other kids during meetings

of the local gas workers' union, of which her father was president. Chanda's paternal grandmother is Selma James, the
Marxist feminist writer and activist who founded Wages for
Housework. And her paternal grandfather by marriage is C.
L. R. James, the socialist scholar who wrote *Black Jacobins*
and collaborated with Grace Lee and Jimmy Boggs and other
giants of the American Left. But theory and ideology didn't
figure much into how Prescod raised her daughter. Instead
she used real-life teachable moments (she remembers the
Rodney King beating as one) to talk with the girl about race,
class, and power.

I can imagine that this is how it will be with us. Something disturbing and illustrative of society's ills will happen,
and I will need to decide whether I want to shelter Is from
the news or discuss it with her. As a toddler, she already asks
"Who's that?" of nearly everyone she sees in the magazines
lying about the house—from *The New Yorker* to *The Nation*
to *Essence*—and on the TV screen. Soon she will begin to
remember and make meaning of our answers. She already
knows that I get excited by the *Sesame Street* clip in which
Grover eats former First Lady Michelle Obama's breakfast,
and her grandmothers taught her to recognize his image and
say the name Barack Obama before she was two years old.
Even if I'm not actively engaging her in activism, the world
will make its way into our home. I will need to decide what
to do with that, how to shape it for her developing mind,
how to know what an age-appropriate rendering of the
truth is, and what is too much. "You want your kids to be
smart, but with that comes a lot of trauma," Bandele tells me.

Accessing the full political power of our mothering means educating the child and knowing how and when to filter out the things they will find too disturbing. How do we live for the we, while also protecting our children's spirits so they're not afraid of the world? There's no one answer, Bandele says. "It's a delicate dance."

Conclusion

I FINISHED WRITING THIS BOOK LATE IN THE SUMMER OF 2018. THE world had recently learned that the US government was taking children, including infants and toddlers, from their parents as they attempted to migrate into the country. It was the summer when Dr. Christine Blasey Ford and others came forward with gripping allegations of sexual assault and boorish behavior perpetrated by Trump's nominee to the US Supreme Court. Despite a wave of protest, he would eventually be narrowly confirmed by the Senate. It was the summer when an off-duty Dallas police officer barged into a black man's apartment, killed him, and then used the defense that she'd thought it was her own apartment and that he was an intruder. In many ways, the summer of 2018 was much like the summer of 2016, when the news cycle left me wanting to crawl into bed and pretend the world wasn't in such terrible shape.

It was different in important ways, too. Two years before, I'd been in my third trimester and anticipating my child's birth. I allowed myself a break from the news for my own health and that of the life developing inside me. By September 2018, I had a two-year-old, and I felt better able to let in and respond to the wider world. Just as writings by other mothers had suggested it would, my skin *did* feel a little thicker, intact again as a barrier. With time, I no longer needed to shield myself from the reality beyond my immediate experience.

Informed by the conversations and research in these pages, I now want to engage in that wider reality with my daughter by my side and in fundamentally different ways. I want to try out solutions to our most pressing problems on a small scale. This is a moment of widespread and profound disappointment. Institutions that many of us have been taught are the building blocks of a democratic society—the electoral process, Congress, the Supreme Court, the office of president—are dysfunctional and unrecognizable. Influencing the state through voting and campaigns of mass persuasion are still important, but mothering and talking to others about their approach to mothering has made me curious about what happens when we join with like-minded people to create the networks and institutions that our families deserve. We need places to practice what we want to see in the world.

In terms of creating spaces that affirm black life, many of us are doing this in small ways already, just as my mother did for me thirty years ago when she put on Whitney Houston's "Greatest Love of All" every morning before we left the house. It's what we do around our dinner tables, at our barbeques and family reunions. We nurture protected spaces where we can relax and express joy and see ourselves as we are, no matter how black life is understood or treated by the broader public.

We are already creating spaces where blood and chosen family can practice a vision that affirms black life. I hope the stories of Little Maroons, the Boggs School, East Bay Meditation Center's family sangha, Detroit Summer, and other community-based institutions described here offer blueprints for additional ways our families might band with others to survive these bleak political times. Those empowered on the global, federal, or state levels may be out of step with and openly hostile to our communities, but what if we gave our best energies and attention to building something new or revitalizing existing community-based projects that are small enough to be responsive and effectively meet our needs?

There are many more examples of politically powerful do-it-yourself efforts throughout history, from the Jane Collective that provided safe abortions in the pre-*Roe* era to the Black Panthers' Free Breakfast for School Children program. Today, communities are trying out transformative justice processes in an effort to prevent harm and interrupt cycles of violence without involving the police or courts. Whether it's divesting from our schools or our food systems or our churches or from limiting narratives about what we're capable of, there's an experiment happening somewhere, and mothers are often in the mix figuring out how to make it work for their families.

The thread that connects these experiments is imagination, the ability of those involved to believe that something better is not only possible in the abstract but within reach and worth the effort right now. At the Allied Media Conference in 2017, I heard an artist and mother named Yasmin Hernandez say that every night before bed she asks her children, "What are you going to dream about tonight?" She wants to get them in the habit of knowing they have some control over their mind's eye. "Revolutionaries are dreamers," she tells them. My favorite people—the ones I am counting on to save us as the world continues to crumble—are the dreamers, the activists who speak beautifully about hope and about the need to vision beyond what we even know to be possible. Maybe one day my daughter will be one of those people. In the meantime, I will do my best to surround her with the ones I know that she can learn from and emulate. She needs to understand the importance of freedom dreams.

Though I've used the words myself throughout this book, I agree with those who argue that the words "left" and "right" no longer accurately describe the divisions in our world.[1] The divisions aren't necessarily between those who believe in the power of the free market versus those who believe in the necessity of a strong social safety net. These competing belief systems still exist, of course, but I think the most important dividing line today is between those who believe our greatest resource is our imagination and those who think unbridled imaginations are dangerous, a threat to existing ways of organizing power. We only have to look at the chorus of "boys will be boys" and "what did she expect?" in response to the #MeToo movement's encouragement that we reimagine gender and power to see how tied some people are to the devil they know.

I aspire to grow my imagination and to strengthen my optimism. I think being a mother and developing these skills alongside my child can help. In these pages I have mentioned my desire to find a place where I could flee with my daughter, a place that will allow her to flourish into her full potential as a black girl. I know that no such perfect place exists. It's not something to find but something to create. I hope this book will contribute to the many thriving conversations about how to do this and that those of us learning how to mother maroons find each other and learn together.

Acknowledgments

I AM GRATEFUL TO EVERYONE WHO SHARED THEIR STORIES. YOU TRUSTED me with your private lives, your hopes, fears, and doubts. May your words inspire others to action and deep reflection. Thank you for offering me your time, your memories, and your expertise.

To the McClains (my mother's sisters and their families), the Pipkins, Dr. Ken Washington, and Deb Wilkinson and family: thank you. You wrap Isobel and me in unmistakable love and care, and we are better for it. Andrea McClain, Joni Pipkins, Amber Pipkins, and Yvonne Copeland came through for us when childcare options looked bleak. Keisha Munson, Jordyn Parks, and Kenya Woodard entertained and cared for Is so that I could work.

Thank you to the teams at Bold Type Books and Hachette. You were dependable, enthusiastic partners in the work. I am especially grateful to Katy O'Donnell for her thoughtful feedback and for her skillful shepherding of the process.

Tanya McKinnon gave me short, doable assignments in the weeks after Isobel was born, and this was the early push I needed. She let me know that in addition to selling the book, she would be a close reader and a fierce advocate. Thank you for following through on your promise.

Taya Kitman and the staff of Type Media Center help make independent journalism possible during these tumultuous times for the profession. Thank you. I am especially grateful to Darren Ankrom, whose careful fact check made the book stronger.

Alessandra Bastagli convinced me that the time for this book was now. Our conversations in the years before I wrote the proposal offered the encouragement I needed. Thank you.

Thank you to adrienne maree brown, Janine de Novais, Fanna Gamal, Alexis Pauline Gumbs, Malika Omawale, Andrea McClain, and Greg Pipkins for reading and reflecting on chapter drafts. ill Weaver's precise transcription saved me a lot of time.

Emily Douglas at *The Nation* edited the article that developed into the first chapter. I appreciate the insights she brought to this story and the many others on which we've collaborated. Katrina Vanden Heuvel, Richard Kim, Kai Wright, and other past and present staffers at the magazine (including many eagle-eyed fact-checkers) have improved my articles and blog posts over the years. I am grateful for the platform *The Nation* provides.

I conducted much of the research on Cincinnati's history in the spring of 2006 as part of Sam Freedman's book-writing seminar at Columbia's journalism school. It was there that I learned how to write a proposal and sustain the focus necessary for a long project. I am also grateful to Sig Gissler, Kevin Coyne, John Dinges, the late Judith Crist, and Addie Rimmer for their guidance. Thank you to Alia Malek, Erika Beras, Zaidee Stavely, David Johnson, Jessica Ramakrishnan, and other j-school '06 classmates who continue to make sure important stories are published and broadcast.

I learned how to report alongside journalists at the *Milwaukee Journal Sentinel*, the *Miami Herald*, the *Cincinnati Herald*, *WireTap*, and the *Indypendent*. *Colorlines* under the leadership of Akiba Solomon has been a consistent home for my articles. Sarah Carr gives me opportunities to keep a hand in education reporting. Kathy Y. Wilson made space for me at *Cincinnati CityBeat* and demanded that I not be boring. Farai Chideya let me tag along on a reporting trip to Florida just after the election of 2000. Thank you to all the editors and colleagues who have patiently taught me the tools of the trade over the years.

I learned the nuts and bolts of advocacy and organizing at Drug Policy Alliance and ColorOfChange. I offer deep gratitude to current and former staffers with whom I've worked at both organizations. The Clark Montessori High School community taught me how to listen to young people. Thank you to the students and adults I worked with during my time there.

AMP family, Jaime Bardacke, Elizabeth Mendez Berry, Dean Blase and family, Dargie Bowersock and the Andersons,

Camp Dennison family, the Goddesses, Jo Griffith, KDub and Kandice Odister, Jamilah King, Gavin Leonard, Mervyn Marcano, Samhita Mukhopadhyay, Kristina Rizga, Sharda Sekaran, Deborah Small, LaWanda Thompson, Jodie Tonita, and many others who connected me to sources and helped shape the ideas expressed here: thank you.

Notes

INTRODUCTION

1. Alexis Pauline Gumbs, China Martens, and Mai'a Williams, *Revolutionary Mothering: Love on the Front Lines* (Oakland: PM Press, 2016), 9.

2. Patricia Hill Collins, "The Meaning of Motherhood in Black Culture and Black Mother/Daughter Relationships," *SAGE: A Scholarly Journal on Black Women* 4, no. 2 (1987): 3–10.

3. Stacey Patton, *Spare the Kids: Why Whupping Won't Save Black America* (Boston: Beacon Press, 2017), 13.

4. Domenico Montanaro, "Here's Just How Little Confidence Americans Have in Political Institutions," *NPR*, January 17, 2018, https://www.npr.org/2018/01/17/578422668/heres-just-how-little-confidence-americans-have-in-political-institutions.

5. Po Bronson and Ashley Merryman, "Even Babies Discriminate: A Nurtureshock Excerpt," *Newsweek*, September 4, 2009, https://www.newsweek.com/even-babies-discriminate-nurtureshock-excerpt-79233; Po Bronson and Ashley Merryman, *NurtureShock: New Thinking about Children* (New York: Twelve, 2009).

CHAPTER 1: BIRTH

1. Institute of Medicine, *Unequal Treatment: Confronting Racial and Ethnic Disparities in Health Care* (Washington, DC: National Academies Press, 2003), https://doi.org/10.17226/10260.

2. Kelly M. Hoffman et al., "Racial Bias in Pain Assessment and Treatment Recommendations, and False Beliefs about Biological Differences between Blacks and Whites," *Proceedings of the National Academy of Sciences of the United States of America* 113, no. 16 (2016): 4296–301; K. A. Schulman, J. A. Berlin, W. Harless, et al., "The Effect of Race and Sex on Physicians' Recommendations for Cardiac Catheterization," *New England Journal of Medicine* 340 (April 8, 1999): 618–26.

3. "Overdue: Medicaid and Private Insurance Coverage of Doula Care to Strengthen Maternal and Infant Health," Childbirth Connection, January 2016, https://transform.childbirthconnection.org/reports/doula/.

4. Colby Itkowitz, "Closure of Two D.C. Maternity Wards Hurts Low-Income Women Most," *Washington Post*, October 28, 2017, https://www.washingtonpost.com/local/closure-of-two-dc-maternity-wards-hurts-low-income-women-most/2017/10/28/753e4dee-ad06-11e7-9e58-e6288544af98_story.html; Sophia Barnes, "Maternity Ward at Southeast D.C. Hospital Will Not Be Reopened," *NBC Washington*, December 14, 2017, https://www.nbcwashington.com/news/health/Southeast-DC-Hospital-Wont-Reopen-Maternity-Ward-After-17M-Subsidy-Request-464210833.html.

5. "Midwives and Women of Color," *Portland Observer*, May 19, 2015, http://portlandobserver.com/news/2015/may/19/midwives-and-women-color/.

6. Midwives Alliance of North America, "Types of Midwives," accessed December 4, 2018, https://mana.org/about-midwives/types-of-midwife; National Midwifery Institute, "Direct-Entry Midwifery," accessed December 4, 2018, https://www.nationalmidwiferyinstitute.com/direct-entry-midwifery/.

CHAPTER 2: HOME

1. Donna Ferguson, "Must Monsters Always Be Male? Huge Gender Bias Revealed in Children's Books," *The Guardian*, January 20, 2018, https://www.theguardian.com/books/2018/jan/21/childrens -books-sexism-monster-in-your-kids-book-is-male.

2. Michael Miner, "Jamie Kalven: The Man with a Lantern," *Chicago Reader*, December 7, 2016, http://people.chicagoreader .com/who/jamie-kalven/profile/.

3. Lauren Weber, "More Than Half of American Babies Are at Risk for Malnourishment," *Huffington Post*, February 3, 2018, https:// www.huffingtonpost.com/entry/malnutrition-children-1000-days _us_5a7138bce4b0be822ba16d1e; Sarah Jane Schwarzenberg and Michael K. Georgieff, "Advocacy for Improving Nutrition in the First 1000 Days to Support Childhood Development and Adult Health," *Pediatrics* 141, no. 2 (February 2018): e20173716, https://doi .org/10.1542/peds.2017-3716.

4. Lydia Nichols, "Anti-Imperialist Parenting: Introduction," March 10, 2018, http://www.lydiaynichols.com/modernmaroon /anti-imperialist-parenting-introduction.

5. Alyssa Knickerbocker, "X-Men," *Tin House*, January 30, 2018, https://tinhouse.com/x-men/.

6. Knickerbocker, "X-Men."

7. Courtney E. Martin, "The Evolving Anxiety of Motherhood," *On Being*, February 1, 2018, https://onbeing.org/blog/courtney -martin-the-evolving-anxiety-of-motherhood/.

8. Jesmyn Ward, "Raising a Black Son in the US: 'He Had Never Taken a Breath, and I Was Already Mourning Him,'" *Guardian*, October 28, 2017, https://www.theguardian.com/lifeandstyle/2017/oct /28/raising-black-son-america.

9. Amy Davidson Sorkin, "Jeff Sessions and Anglo-Americanism," *The New Yorker*, February 13, 2018, https://www.newyorker.com /news/daily-comment/jeff-sessions-and-anglo-americanism.

10. Phillip Atiba Goff et al., "The Essence of Innocence: Consequences of Dehumanizing Black Children," *Journal of Personality and Social Psychology* 106, no. 4 (February 2014): 526–545, https://doi.org/10.1037/a0035663.

11. Rochaun Meadows-Fernandez, "After Charlottesville: We Need to Start 'Spoiling' Our Black Children," *Washington Post*, August 15, 2017, https://www.washingtonpost.com/news/parenting/wp/2017/08/15/we-need-to-start-spoiling-our-black-children/?utm_term=.b55c1ea1abf1.

CHAPTER 3: FAMILY

1. "Obama's Father's Day Remarks," *New York Times*, June 15, 2008, https://www.nytimes.com/2008/06/15/us/politics/15text-obama.html.

2. "Full Transcript of the Second Presidential Debate," *New York Times*, October 16, 2012, https://www.nytimes.com/2012/10/16/us/politics/transcript-of-the-second-presidential-debate-in-hempstead-ny.html.

3. Jasmine Tucker and Caitlin Lowell, "National Snapshot: Poverty among Women & Families, 2015," National Women's Law Center, September 14, 2016, https://nwlc.org/resources/national-snapshot-poverty-among-women-families-2015/.

4. Marcia J. Carlson, Sara S. McLanahan, and Jeanne Brooks-Gunn, "Coparenting and Nonresident Fathers' Involvement with Young Children after a Nonmarital Birth," *Demography* 45, no. 2 (May 2008): 461–488, https://doi.org/10.1353/dem.0.0007.

5. Justin Wolfers, David Leonhardt, and Kevin Quealy, "1.5 Million Missing Black Men," *New York Times*, April 20, 2015, https://www.nytimes.com/interactive/2015/04/20/upshot/missing-black-men.html.

6. Daphne Lofquist et al., "Households and Families: 2010," *2010 Census Briefs*, April 2012, https://www.census.gov/prod/cen2010/briefs/c2010br-14.pdf.

7. Drug Policy Alliance, "A Brief History of the Drug War," http://www.drugpolicy.org/issues/brief-history-drug-war; Peter Wagner and Wendy Sawyer, "Mass Incarceration: The Whole Pie 2018," Prison Policy Initiative, March 18, 2018, https://www.prison policy.org/reports/pie2018.html.

8. Angela Davis, "Reflections on the Black Woman's Role in the Community of Slaves," *The Massachusetts Review* 13, no. 1/2 (1972): 82–83, http://www.jstor.org/stable/25088201; Andrea O'Reilly, *Toni Morrison and Motherhood: A Politics of the Heart* (Albany: State University of New York Press, 2004), 1–20, https://www.sunypress .edu/pdf/60924.pdf.

9. Carol Stack, *All Our Kin: Strategies for Survival in a Black Community* (New York: Harper & Row, 1974).

10. Stack, *All Our Kin*, 124.

11. Mark Leviton, "The Kids Are All Right," *The Sun*, February 2016, https://www.thesunmagazine.org/issues/482/the-kids-are-all-right; Michael Erard, "The Only Baby Book You'll Ever Need," *New York Times*, January 31, 2015, https://www.nytimes.com/2015/02/01 /opinion/sunday/the-only-baby-book-youll-ever-need.html.

12. Lake Research Partners and Family Story, "Online Survey Briefing," November 28, 2017, https://familystoryproject.org/wp-content /uploads/2018/10/LRP-Memo_Key-Findings_2017.07.25.pdf.

13. Audre Lorde, "Man Child," *Sister Outsider: Essays and Speeches* (Trumansburg: Crossing Press, 1984), 79.

14. Lorde, "Man Child," 76.

15. Amber J. Phillips (@AmberJPhillips), Twitter, June 17, 2018, https://twitter.com/amberjphillips/status/1008344289770967040.

16. P. H. Collins, "The Meaning of Motherhood in Black Culture and Black Mother/Daughter Relationships," *SAGE: A Scholarly Journal on Black Women* 4, no. 2 (1987): 3–10.

17. Michele Wallace, *Black Macho and the Myth of the Superwoman* (New York: Dial Press, 1979), *11, 31*.

18. Sara McLanahan and Christopher Jencks, "Was Moynihan Right? What Happens to Children of Unmarried Mothers,"

EducationNext 15, no. 2 (Spring 2015): 14–20, http://educationnext
.org/was-moynihan-right/.

19. Katherine Boo, "The Marriage Cure," *The New Yorker*, August 18, 2003, https://www.newyorker.com/magazine/2003/08/18/the -marriage-cure.

20. Boo, "Marriage Cure."

21. David Brady et al., "Single Mothers Are Not the Problem," *New York Times*, February 10, 2018, https://www.nytimes.com/2018 /02/10/opinion/sunday/single-mothers-poverty.html.

22. Virginia Kruta, "I'm a Conservative, and I Went to an Alexandria Ocasio-Cortez Rally," *Daily Caller*, July 23, 2018, https://dailycaller .com/2018/07/23/conservative-alexandria-ocasio-cortez-rally/.

23. O'Reilly, *Politics of the Heart*, 5–6.

24. Jo Jones et al., "Fathers' Involvement with Their Children: United States, 2006–2010," *National Health Statistics Reports* no. 71, December 20, 2013, https://www.cdc.gov/nchs/data/nhsr/nhsr071 .pdf; Charles M. Blow, "Black Dads Are Doing Best of All," *New York Times*, June 8, 2015, https://www.nytimes.com/2015/06/08/opinion /charles-blow-black-dads-are-doing-the-best-of-all.html.

25. Emma, "You Should've Asked," May 20, 2017, https://english .emmaclit.com/2017/05/20/you-shouldve-asked/.

26. Davis, "Reflections," 87.

27. Travis L. Dixon, "A Dangerous Distortion of Our Families: Representations of Families, by Race, in News and Opinion Media," Study commissioned by Color of Change and Family Story, December 2017, https://s3.amazonaws.com/coc-dangerousdisruption/full -report.pdf.

28. Jasmine Tucker and Caitlin Lowell, "National Snapshot: Poverty among Women & Families, 2015," National Women's Law Center, September 2016, https://nwlc.org/wp-content/uploads/2016/09 /Poverty-Snapshot-Factsheet-2016.pdf.

29. asha bandele, *Something Like Beautiful: One Single Mother's Story* (New York: HarperCollins, 2009).

30. Aya de Leon, "Deciding to Marry Myself," *Essence*, June 1997, https://ayadeleon.files.wordpress.com/2015/02/essence-interiors -jpeg.jpg.

CHAPTER 4: PLAY

1. Lauren Sandler explores these misconceptions in *One and Only: The Freedom of Having an Only Child, and the Joy of Being One* (New York: Simon & Schuster, 2014).

2. James P. Comer and Alvin F. Poussaint, *Raising Black Children: Two Leading Psychiatrists Confront the Educational, Social and Emotional Problems Facing Black Children* (New York: Plume, 1992).

3. Erika Christakis, *The Importance of Being Little: What Young Children Really Need from Grownups* (New York: Penguin, 2016), 84–85.

4. Christakis, *Importance of Being Little*, 81.

5. Valerie Strauss, "250 Preschoolers Suspended or Expelled Every School Day, According to New Analysis," *Washington Post*, November 7, 2017, https://www.washingtonpost.com/news/answer -sheet/wp/2017/11/07/250-preschoolers-suspended-or-expelled -every-school-day-new-analysis.

6. Christakis, *Importance of Being Little*, 79.

CHAPTER 5: BELONGING

1. "Presidential Result," *CNN*, https://www.cnn.com/election /2016/results/states/ohio.

2. John Larson, "Behind the Death of Timothy Thomas," *Dateline NBC*, updated April 10, 2004, http://www.nbcnews.com /id/4703574/ns/dateline_nbc-dateline_specials/t/behind-death -timothy-thomas/#.W8NMoRNKiCQ.

3. "Cincinnati Riot of 1829," Charles H. Wright Museum of African American History, http://ugrr.thewright.org/53-view-other -media.html?id=3433&title=cincinnati_riot_of_1829; Interview

with Charles F. Casey-Leininger, PhD, Department of History, University of Cincinnati, March 17, 2006; "Cincinnati Rally by Klan Draws 1,500 Hecklers," *Associated Press*, December 23, 1990, http://articles.latimes.com/1990-12-23/news/mn-9880_1_klan-member; David Margolick, "Klan's Plan for Cross Stokes Anger in Cincinnati," *New York Times*, December 18, 1992, https://www.nytimes.com/1992/12/18/news/klan-s-plan-for-cross-stokes-anger-in-cincinnati.html; "Klan Cross Erected in Cincinnati," *Chicago Tribune*, December 20, 1993, http://www.chicagotribune.com/news/ct-xpm-1993-12-20-9312210203-story.html.

4. Stephanie Dunlap, "Return and Retrieve," *Cincinnati CityBeat*, May 5, 2004, https://www.citybeat.com/home/article/13020760/cover-story-return-and-retrieve.

5. Grace Lee Boggs, *Living for Change: An Autobiography* (Minneapolis: University of Minnesota Press, 1998), 232.

6. Jason Johnson, "Why White Americans Call the Police on Black People in Public Spaces," interview by Ari Shapiro, *All Things Considered*, NPR, May 15, 2018, audio, 4:35, https://www.npr.org/2018/05/15/611389765/why-white-americans-call-the-police-on-black-people-in-public-spaces.

7. Portia Adams, "Self-Esteem Research in Black Communities: 'On the Whole, I'm Satisfied with Myself,'" *African American Research Perspectives* 10, no. 1 (Spring/Summer 2004): 66–78, http://www.rcgd.isr.umich.edu/prba/perspectives/springsummer2004/adams.pdf; Suzanne Daley, "Little Girls Lose Their Self-Esteem Way to Adolescence, Study Finds," *New York Times*, January 9, 1991, https://www.nytimes.com/1991/01/09/education/little-girls-lose-their-self-esteem-way-to-adolescence-study-finds.html.

8. Boggs, *Living for Change*, 233.

CHAPTER 6: SCHOOL

1. "Are Private Schools Immoral? A Conversation with Nikole Hannah-Jones about Race, Education, and Hypocrisy," interview by

Jeffrey Goldberg, *The Atlantic Interview*, December 14, 2017, https://
www.theatlantic.com/education/archive/2017/12/progressives
-are-undermining-public-schools/548084/.

2. Shelly Hagan and Wei Lu, "America's 100 Richest Places,"
Bloomberg, March 5, 2018, https://www.bloomberg.com/graphics
/2018-hundred-richest-places/.

3. Patrick Sharkey, "Neighborhoods and the Black-White Mobility Gap," *Economic Mobility Project: An Initiative of the Pew Charitable
Trusts* (July 2009): 3, 6, https://www.pewtrusts.org/~/media/legacy
/uploadedfiles/wwwpewtrustsorg/reports/economic_mobility
/pewsharkeyv12pdf.pdf.

4. Emily Badger et al., "Extensive Data Shows Punishing Reach
of Racism for Black Boys," *New York Times*, March 19, 2018, https://
www.nytimes.com/interactive/2018/03/19/upshot/race-class
-white-and-black-men.html; Ralph Richard Banks, "An End to the
Class vs. Race Debate," *New York Times*, March 21, 2018, https://
www.nytimes.com/2018/03/21/opinion/class-race-social-mobility.
html; Matthew Bloch et al., "An Extremely Detailed Map of the 2016
Election," *New York Times*, July 25, 2018, https://www.nytimes.com
/interactive/2018/upshot/election-2016-voting-precinct-maps.html.

5. "School Segregation in 2018 with Nikole Hannah-Jones,"
interview by Chris Hayes, *Why Is This Happening? With Chris Hayes*,
July 31, 2018, audio, 58:50, https://www.stitcher.com/podcast
/msnbc/why-is-this-happening/e/55572429?autoplay=true.

6. Eula Biss, "Let's Talk about Whiteness," interview by Krista
Tippett, *On Being*, January 19, 2017, audio, https://onbeing.org
/programs/eula-biss-lets-talk-about-whiteness-jan2017/; Eula Biss,
"White Debt," *New York Times*, December 2, 2015, https://www
.nytimes.com/2015/12/06/magazine/white-debt.html/.

7. Twilight Greenaway, "The Truth about 'Underperforming
Schools' That Parents Don't Want to Admit," *Scary Mommy*, https://
www.scarymommy.com/underperforming-schools-segregated
-education/; Zaidee Stavely, "Two Moms Choose between Separate
and Unequal Schools in Oakland," *KQED*, August 30, 2016, https://

www.kqed.org/news/11059974/two-moms-choose-between
-separate-and-unequal-schools-in-oakland.

8. Courtney E. Martin, "Parenting Like a Citizen," *On Being*, April 8, 2016, https://onbeing.org/blog/parenting-like-a-citizen/.

9. Emily Gersema, "White Families with Children Are Drawn to Less Diverse Neighborhoods, Schools," *University of Southern California News*, March 22, 2017, https://news.usc.edu/118827/white-families-with-children-are-drawn-to-less-diverse-neighborhoods-schools/.

10. Mackenzie Mays, "The Complexity of Covering School Segregation," *Education Writers Association*, July 11, 2016, https://www.ewa.org/blog-educated-reporter/complexity-covering-school-segregation.

11. "Prof. R. L'Heureux Lewis-McCoy Reveals 'Inequality in the Promised Land,'" June 16, 2014, *Colin Powell School for Civic and Global Leadership at the City College of New York*, https://colinpowellcenter1.wordpress.com/2014/06/16/prof-r-lheureux-lewis-mccoy-reveals-inequality-in-the-promised-land/.

12. Susan Dynarski, "Why Talented Black and Hispanic Students Can Go Undiscovered," *New York Times*, April 8, 2016, https://www.nytimes.com/2016/04/10/upshot/why-talented-black-and-hispanic-students-can-go-undiscovered.html.

13. Interview with Fanna Gamal, June 20, 2018.

14. Paul L. Morgan and George Farkas, "Is Special Education Racist?" *New York Times*, June 24, 2015, https://www.nytimes.com/2015/06/24/opinion/is-special-education-racist.html; Nora Gordon, "Race, Poverty, and Interpreting Overrepresentation in Special Education," Brookings, September 20, 2017, https://www.brookings.edu/research/race-poverty-and-interpreting-overrepresentation-in-special-education/.

15. Lee Romney, "This East Bay School District's Success in Getting Kids to School Is a Model for the State," KALW, December 14, 2017, http://www.kalw.org/post/east-bay-school-district-s

-success-getting-kids-school-model-state#stream/0; "California School Dashboard," *California Department of Education*, https://www.caschooldashboard.org.

16. Amine Ouazad, "Assessed by a Teacher Like Me: Race, Gender, and Subjective Evaluations," INSEAD Working Paper No. 2008/57/EPS (September 12, 2008), http://dx.doi.org/10.2139/ssrn.1267109.

17. Stacy Teicher Khadaroo, "Restorative Justice: One High School's Path to Reducing Suspensions by Half," *Christian Science Monitor*, March 31, 2013, https://www.csmonitor.com/USA/Education/2013/0331/Restorative-justice-One-high-school-s-path-to-reducing-suspensions-by-half.

18. Susan Frey, "Oakland Ends Suspensions for Willful Defiance, Funds Restorative Justice," *EdSource*, May 14, 2015, https://edsource.org/2015/oakland-ends-suspensions-for-willful-defiance-funds-restorative-justice/79731; Melinda D. Anderson, "Will School-Discipline Reform Actually Change Anything?," *The Atlantic*, September 14, 2015, https://www.theatlantic.com/education/archive/2015/09/will-school-discipline-reform-actually-change-anything/405157/.

CHAPTER 7: BODY

1. Eleanor Morrison and Faye Orlove, *C Is for Consent* (Los Angeles: Phonics with Finn, 2018).

2. "2018 Sex Ed State Legislative Mid-Year Report," *Sexuality Information and Education Council of the United States*, September 5, 2018, 3, https://siecus.org/wp-content/uploads/2018/09/2018_mid-year_State_Leg_9-5-18_Update.pdf; "19 Critical Sexual Education Topics," *School Health Profiles*, Centers for Disease Control and Prevention, 2016, https://www.cdc.gov/healthyyouth/data/profiles/pdf/19_criteria_landscape.pdf; "Sex Education Linked to Delay in First Sex," Guttmacher Institute, March 8, 2012, https://www.guttmacher

.org/news-release/2012/sex-education-linked-delay-first-sex; Sarah Shapiro and Catherine Brown, "Sex Education Standards across the States," Center for American Progress, May 9, 2018, https://www.americanprogress.org/issues/education-k-12/reports/2018/05/09/450158/sex-education-standards-across-states/; "Instruction in Venereal Disease Education Emphasizing Abstinence," Ohio Revised Code, http://codes.ohio.gov/orc/3313.6011.

3. Emily F. Rothman and Avanti Adhia, "Adolescent Pornography Use and Dating Violence among a Sample of Primarily Black and Hispanic, Urban-Residing, Underage Youth," *Behavioral Sciences* 6, no. 1 (2016): 1, https://doi.org/10.3390/bs6010001; Maggie Jones, "What Teenagers Are Learning from Online Porn," *New York Times*, February 7, 2018, https://www.nytimes.com/2018/02/07/magazine/teenagers-learning-online-porn-literacy-sex-education.html.

4. "Given & Chosen: Talking to Family about Sexuality," Illinois Caucus for Adolescent Health, June 2013, https://www.icah.org/blog/participatory-action-research; "ICAH Youth Research on Given and Chosen Families," YouTube, March 6, 2013, https://www.youtube.com/watch?v=fR1KjYY0IMM&feature=c4-overview&list=UUB-_Nr38blLUC-pJAI_TQlw.

5. Jennifer Wright (@JenAshleyWright), Twitter, November 9, 2017, https://twitter.com/jenashleywright/status/928740631035437057?lang=en.

6. "bell hooks on the Roots of Male Violence against Women," interview by David Remnick, *The New Yorker Radio Hour*, November 17, 2017, audio, 9:54, http://www.wnyc.org/story/bell-hooks-roots-male-violence-against-women/.

7. Jenifer Lewis, "Wheatgrass in Your Ass," interview by Tracy Clayton and Heben Nigatu, *Another Round*, November 22, 2017, audio, 53:34, https://www.acast.com/anotherround/episode-110-wheatgrass-in-your-ass-with-jenifer-lewis.

8. Christina Maxouris and Saeed Ahmed, "Only These 8 States Require Sex Education Classes to Mention Consent," CNN, September 29, 2018, https://www.cnn.com/2018/09/29/health /sex-education-consent-in-public-schools-trnd/index.html.

9. Richard Rohr, "Living in Deep Time," interview by Krista Tippett, *On Being*, April 13, 2017, audio, 51:53, https://onbeing.org /programs/richard-rohr-living-in-deep-time-apr2017/.

10. "New CDC Analysis Shows Steep and Sustained Increases in STDs in Recent Years," Centers for Disease Control and Prevention, August 28, 2018, https://www.cdc.gov/nchhstp/news-room/2018/press-release-2018-std-prevention-conference.html; "Adolescents and Young Adults," Centers for Disease Control and Prevention, last modified December 8, 2017, https://www.cdc.gov /std/life-stages-populations/adolescents-youngadults.htm; "STDs in Racial and Ethnic Minorities," Centers for Disease Control and Prevention, last modified September 26, 2017, https://www.cdc.gov /std/stats16/minorities.htm; "HIV among African American Youth," Centers for Disease Control and Prevention, last modified February 2014, https://www.cdc.gov/nchhstp/newsroom/docs/factsheets /archive/cdc-youth-aas-508.pdf.

11. Interview with Stephanie Teal, August 18, 2015.

12. "Champagne Papi," *Atlanta*, Season 2, Episode 7, broadcast April 12, 2018, https://www.springfieldspringfield.co.uk/view _episode_scripts.php?tv-show=atlanta-2016&episode=s02e07.

13. Pam Belluck, "Trump Administration Pushes Abstinence in Teen Pregnancy Programs," *New York Times*, April 23, 2018, https://www.nytimes.com/2018/04/23/health/trump -teen-pregnancy-abstinence.html; Michelle Andrews, "Trump's Redirection of Family Planning Funds Could Undercut STD Fight," *NPR*, June 12, 2018, https://www.npr.org/sections/health -shots/2018/06/12/618902785/trumps-redirection-of-fam-ily-planning-funds-could-undercut-std-fight; Lena H. Sun and

Juliet Eilperin, "CDC Gets List of Forbidden Words: Fetus, Transgender, Diversity," *Washington Post*, December 15, 2017, https://www.washingtonpost.com/national/health-science/cdc-gets-list-of-forbidden-words-fetus-transgender-diversity/2017/12/15/f503837a-e1cf-11e7-89e8-edec16379010_story.html.

14. Roberta A. Downing et al., "Intersections of Ethnicity and Social Class in Provider Advice Regarding Reproductive Health," *American Journal of Public Health* 97, no. 10 (2007): 1803–1807, https://doi.org/10.2105/AJPH.2006.092585; "Provider Advice to Women May Vary by Women's Social Class and Ethnicity," Guttmacher Institute, March 10, 2008, https://www.guttmacher.org/journals/psrh/2008/provider-advice-women-may-vary-womens-social-class-and-ethnicity; Christine Dehlendorf et al., "Recommendations for Intrauterine Contraception: A Randomized Trial of the Effects of Patients' Race/Ethnicity and Socioeconomic Status," *American Journal of Obstetrics and Gynecology* 203, no. 4 (2010): 319.e1-8, https://doi.org/10.1016/j.ajog.2010.05.009.

CHAPTER 8: SPIRIT

1. Adam Liptak and Michael Wines, "Strict North Carolina Voter ID Law Thwarted after Supreme Court Rejects Case," *New York Times*, May 15, 2017, https://www.nytimes.com/2017/05/15/us/politics/voter-id-laws-supreme-court-north-carolina.html.

2. Joan Halifax, "Buoyancy Rather Than Burnout in Our Lives," interview by Krista Tippett, *On Being*, October 12, 2017, audio, 52:11, https://onbeing.org/programs/joan-halifax-buoyancy-rather-than-burnout-in-our-lives-oct2017/.

3. Nsenga Warfield-Coppock, "The Rites of Passage Movement: A Resurgence of African-Centered Practices for Socializing African American Youth," *Journal of Negro Education* 61, no. 4 (1992): 471–482. https://doi.org/10.2307/2295365.

CHAPTER 9: POWER

1. Patricia Hill Collins, "Shifting the Center: Race, Class, and Feminist Theorizing about Motherhood," in *Mothering: Ideology, Experience and Agency*, ed. Evelyn Nakano Glenn, Grace Chang, and Linda Forcey (New York: Routledge, 1994), 373.

2. Larissa MacFarquhar, "Chimamanda Ngozi Adichie Comes to Terms with Global Fame," *The New Yorker*, June 4 & 11, 2018, https://www.newyorker.com/magazine/2018/06/04/chimamanda-ngozi-adichie-comes-to-terms-with-global-fame.

3. Dani McClain, "The Bitter 'Black Lives Matter' Fight You Should Know About," *Talking Points Memo*, March 13, 2015, https://talkingpointsmemo.com/theslice/black-friday-14-oakland.

4. Olivia Allen-Price, "How Many Are Being Displaced by Gentrification in Oakland," *KQED*, February 9, 2017, https://www.kqed.org/news/11307279/how-many-are-being-displaced-by-gentrification-in-oakland.

5. Susan Chira, "Driven by South's Past, Black Women Seek Votes and a New Future," *New York Times*, October 4, 2018, https://www.nytimes.com/2018/10/04/us/politics/black-women-voters-south.html; Jessica Taylor, "Georgia's Stacey Abrams Admits Defeat, Says Kemp Used 'Deliberate' Suppression to Win," NPR, November 16, 2018, https://www.npr.org/2018/11/16/668753230/democrat-stacey-abrams-ends-bid-for-georgia-governor-decrying-suppression.

6. Will Drabold, "Read What the Mothers of the Movement Said at the Democratic Convention," *Time*, July 27, 2016, http://time.com/4424704/dnc-mothers-movement-transcript-speech-video/; Lucy Kay McBath (@lucymcbath), Twitter, November 23, 2017, https://twitter.com/lucymcbath/status/933808010954199040?lang=en.

7. Allyson Chiu and Samantha Schmidt, "Lucy McBath: Moved to Run for Congress by Son's Fatal Shooting, She Just Won Her Primary," *Washington Post*, July 25, 2018, https://www

.washingtonpost.com/news/morning-mix/wp/2018/07/25/lucy
-mcbath-moved-to-run-for-congress-by-sons-fatal-shooting-she
-just-won-her-primary/?noredirect=on&utm_term=.aa4f745ce08a.

8. Eric Bradner and Kyung Lah, "Gun Control Activist Lucy McBath Wins Democratic Nomination in Georgia's House Race, CNN Projects," CNN, July 24, 2018, https://www.cnn .com/2018/07/24/politics/lucy-mcbath-georgia-runoff/index. html; "Mayoral Election in Oakland, California (2018)," Ballotpedia, https://ballotpedia.org/Mayoral_election_in_Oakland,_California _(2018); Jamilah King, "A White Man Shot and Killed Her Only Son. Now Lucy McBath Is Running So It Doesn't Happen to Anyone Else," *Mother Jones*, March/April 2018, https://www.motherjones.com /politics/2018/02/a-white-man-shot-and-killed-her-only-son-now -lucy-mcbath-is-running-so-it-doesnt-happen-to-anyone-else/; "A Rising Tide? The Changing Demographics on Our Ballots," *Reflective Democracy Campaign*, October 2018, https://wholeads.us /2018-report/.

9. Evan Osnos, "Doomsday Prep for the Super-Rich," *The New Yorker*, January 30, 2017, https://www.newyorker.com/magazine /2017/01/30/doomsday-prep-for-the-super-rich.

10. Aaron Smith, "Smartphone Ownership 2013," Pew Research Center, http://www.pewinternet.org/2013/06/05/smartphone -ownership-2013/; Jean M. Twenge, "Have Smartphones Destroyed a Generation?" *The Atlantic*, September 2017, https://www.theatlantic .com/magazine/archive/2017/09/has-the-smartphone-destroyed-a -generation/534198/.

11. "Open Admissions at CUNY: Review," FairTest, https://www .fairtest.org/open-admissions-cuny-review.

12. "Women, Welfare, and Poverty," *The Spirit of Houston*, March 1978, http://www.everymothernetwork.net/historic-welfare -resolution-passed-at-the-1977-houston-womens-conference/; Mar- jorie Spruill, "Women Unite! Lessons from 1977 for 2017," *Process:*

A Blog for American History, January 20, 2017, http://www.process history.org/women-unite-spruill/.

13. Kirk Siegler, "Families of LA Serial Killer's Victims Still Await Closure," *NPR*, May 2, 2016, https://www.npr.org/2016/05/02/476017102/6-years-later-families-of-la-serial-killers-victims-still-await-closure.

14. Nico Pitney, "Meet the 63rd Black Woman in American History with a Physics Ph.D.," *Huffington Post*, June 24, 2015, https://www.huffingtonpost.com/2015/06/24/chanda-prescod-weinstein_n_7574020.html.

15. Cat Brooks, "For Oscar," YouTube, October 22, 2015, https://www.youtube.com/watch?v=pJlYQpAztao.

16. Matthew Artz, "Black Lives Matter Leader Cat Brooks Playing the Role of Her Life," *East Bay Times*, July 7, 2015, https://www.eastbaytimes.com/2015/07/07/black-lives-matter-leader-cat-brooks-playing-the-role-of-her-life/.

CONCLUSION

1. Anne Applebaum, "Journalist: Poland's Shift toward Authoritarianism Is a 'Red Flag' for Democracy," interview by Terry Gross, *Fresh Air*, NPR, September 27, 2018, audio, 36:49, https://www.npr.org/2018/09/27/652127648/journalist-polands-shift-toward-authoritarianism-is-a-red-flag-for-democracy.

DANI MCCLAIN reports on race, reproductive health, and activism. She is a contributing writer at *The Nation* and a fellow at the Nation Institute. McClain's writing has appeared in outlets including *Slate*, *Talking Points Memo*, *Colorlines*, EBONY.com, *The Rumpus*, and *Guernica*. She reported on education while on staff at the *Milwaukee Journal Sentinel* and has worked as a strategist with organizations including Color of Change and the Drug Policy Alliance. McClain lives in Cincinnati with her family.